RockRecipes 3

Even more Great Food and Photos

From My Newfoundland Kitchen

Barry C. Parsons

D1210832

RockRecipes

Also Available

Rock Recipes

The *Best* Food From My Newfoundland Kitchen

BARRY C. PARSONS

Rock Recipes 2

More Great Food and Photos
From My Newfoundland Kitchen

BARRY C. PARSONS

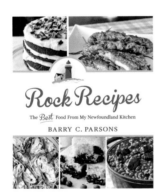

Rock Recipes
CHRISTMAS

YOUR COMPLETE GUIDE TO A DELICIOUS HOLIDAY SEASON

BARRY C. PARSONS

Rock Recipes
COOKIES

A DECADE OF DECADENT RECIPES

BARRY C. PARSONS

BREAKWATER
P.O. Box 2188 | St. John's | NL | Canada | A1C 6E6
www.breakwaterbooks.com

Breakwater Books is committed to choosing papers and materials for our books that help to protect our environment. To this end, this book is printed on a recycled paper that is certified by the Forest Stewardship Council of Canada.

A CIP catalogue record for this book is available from Library and Archives Canada.

ISBN 978-1-55081-856-7

We acknowledge the financial support of the Government of Canada and the Government of Newfoundland and Labrador through the Department of Tourism, Culture and Recreation for our publishing activities.

PRINTED AND BOUND IN CANADA

For

Olivia and Noah,
who make me proud every day.

contents

Well, it's been quite a ride over the last thirteen years since I first started *Rock Recipes*. There have been so many milestones along the way, I can hardly count them. And they still keep coming, as *Rock Recipes* continues to grow year after year.

Traffic on the website has grown past any expectations, with records falling year after year. The site can see up to an amazing 3 million page views a month now, and we are about to hit 1,800 recipe posts since 2007.

That work represents many thousands of hours of cooking, baking, photographing, editing, and writing. The rewards, though, have far outweighed the effort.

The thousands of messages of encouragement from fans of *Rock Recipes*, sharing their culinary success, are what has kept me interested and inspired to continue.

I am thankful every day to the followers of my website and those who buy my cookbooks. Without all of you, this endeavour would likely have ended years ago. You are indeed the inspiration that keeps me moving forward.

It again seems a little surreal to be sitting here writing the introduction to my fifth cookbook! That would have seemed inconceivable in the first few years of writing my blog, but here I sit, doing just that.

It's actually been a full five years since I published a general cookbook, though, since *Rock Recipes 2* hit the shelves back in 2015. In the interim, I wrote both a Christmas cookbook and a cookies cookbook, but the time seems right to add *Rock Recipes 3* to the family.

There have been hundreds of new recipes added to my blog over those five years, so there was a big pool to draw from. Cutting all of those down to just one hundred for this book was quite the challenge.

The past five years have also seen some of the most successful and popular recipes on *Rock Recipes* since its September 2007 inception. Many of them have been seen millions of times online, so yes, it was high time that they be included in a new cookbook.

So, I hope you enjoy thumbing through the pages of this book for cooking and baking ideas to share with your family and friends. Real food recipes for real people is still what *Rock Recipes* is all about, and I hope that sharing them around the table with those you love makes many happy memories for years to come.

After thirteen years online, chicken dishes continue to be the most popular and most searched-for recipes on our website. In fact, chicken recipes are searched for more than all other meats combined.

With that kind of popularity, you need plenty of tasty ideas to cook this versatile protein. From Sunday dinner favourites like Lemon Thyme Roast Chicken, to spicy numbers like Peri-Peri Chicken and our recently popular oven-baked Honey Garlic BBQ Chicken, you're sure to find plenty of tasty inspiration for chicken dinners galore.

chicken

Smokin' Summer Spice Dry Rub

PREP TIME **10** MINUTES | SERVES **100** SERVINGS OF **1** TEASPOON EACH

The only barbecue spice dry rub you will need for the entire grilling season and year-round. It's a versatile and delicious blend of smokey herbs and spices that's delicious on burgers, chicken, steak, beef brisket, pork—absolutely anything that comes off of your grill or out of your backyard smoker. This is a spice mix we always have on hand. It's featured in several recipes in this book, so refer back here when you need it.

6	tbsp	brown sugar
3	tbsp	kosher salt
3	tbsp	onion powder
3	tbsp	paprika
2	tbsp	chili powder
2	tbsp	smoked paprika
1	tbsp	black pepper
1	tbsp	chipotle powder
1	tbsp	ground coriander
1	tbsp	ground nutmeg
1	tbsp	ground oregano
1	tbsp	ground thyme
1	tbsp	powdered ginger
1	tsp	cinnamon
1	tsp	ground cumin

1. Mix together well and store in an airtight container in a cool place. I like to mix it by pulsing it together in the food processor. This ensures it is very well blended and also breaks up any lumps in the brown sugar.

Peri-Peri Sauce *for* Portuguese Chicken

PREP TIME **30 MINUTES** | COOK TIME **30 MINUTES** | SERVES **16 (ABOUT 3 CUPS OF SAUCE)**

2 large red bell peppers, char grilled

1 large red onion, char grilled

½ cup lemon juice

¼ cup red wine vinegar, or apple cider vinegar

10 small red Thai chilis, roughly chopped (more, to taste, for hotter sauce)

4 cloves garlic, minced

zest of 1 lemon, finely grated

1½ tsp dried oregano

1½ tsp kosher salt

1½ tsp smoked paprika, or plain paprika

1 tsp black pepper

2 bay leaves

TO FINISH THE SAUCE WHEN IT IS COOKED

¼ cup lemon juice

¼ cup red wine vinegar, or apple cider vinegar

zest of 1 lemon, finely minced

½ cup extra virgin olive oil

Peri-peri sauce is garlicky, spicy, lemony, tangy, and utterly addictive. Originating in Portugal with African influence, this sauce is at the centre of the incredible success of the Nando's restaurant franchise in many parts of the world and particularly in the UK.

This incredibly addictive homemade version is perfect to bottle and have on hand for chicken, pork, wings, shrimp, or seafood. It is now a staple of the summer grilling season in our home.

---

1. Start by roasting the red peppers and onion. This can be done on a gas grill, under the broiler, or on a cast iron grill pan. You want to get good char marks on the outside of the peppers and onion. Don't worry if they are not fully cooked, they will get fully cooked in the sauce.

2. Chop the peppers and onion and add them to a food processor or blender. You can use an immersion blender if that is all you have on hand; just take the time to get the ingredients well puréed.

3. Add the lemon juice, red wine vinegar, red Thai chilis, garlic, lemon zest, oregano, salt, smoked paprika, and pepper to the food processor with the grilled onions and peppers and purée until smooth.

4. Transfer the sauce to a medium saucepan, add the bay leaves, and simmer slowly for 20-30 minutes.

5. Let the sauce cool to warm. Remove the bay leaves then return the sauce to the food processor.

6. Add the additional lemon juice, red wine vinegar, and lemon zest. Purée for another few minutes until very smooth. Slowly add the olive oil in a thin stream as the processor is running.

to make peri-peri chicken >

1. Brush a little of the sauce onto all sides of the chicken. You can use bone-in, skin-on chicken or boneless, skinless chicken. Place the chicken pieces in a glass dish and cover with plastic wrap. Let the chicken marinate for several hours or overnight.

2. Grill over low heat on a gas grill until fully cooked, brushing on additional sauce in the last five to ten minutes of cook time. Serve with extra sauce for dipping at the table.

Lemon Thyme Roast Chicken

PREP TIME 20 MINUTES | **COOK TIME 1 HOUR 30 MINUTES** | **SERVES 4**

4 tbsp anise seeds,
   or 4 whole star anise

4 tbsp dried thyme

3 tbsp peppercorns

1 tsp whole cloves

1 cup boiling water

6 litres water

1 cup kosher salt

¾ cup brown sugar
(you can experiment with
flavours by using equal
amounts of other sugars like
honey, maple, or molasses)

1 onion, chopped

4 cloves garlic, chopped

juice of 1 whole lemon + peel

few sprigs fresh thyme if you
have them

one 3-4-pound chicken
(you can brine 2 chickens at
once; see note)

2 tbsp olive oil

fresh thyme, chopped, to
season the skin (dried can be
substituted)

1 small whole lemon

about 6 sprigs fresh thyme

4 cloves garlic, peeled

Brined in lemon, garlic, spices, and thyme, this is a super juicy and flavourful roast chicken recipe that makes the perfect Sunday dinner or for any day of the week.

I like brining poultry because it infuses extra juiciness and deeply seasons the meat.

Don't fret, though, if you don't want to. This recipe will still be plenty flavourful even if you skip the brining process. Lots of people have written to me over the past few years to say just that.

---

1. In a small bowl combine anise, thyme, peppercorns, cloves, and boiling water. Set aside to steep for a few minutes while you prepare the rest of the brine.

2. In a large bowl combine 6 litres water, salt, sugar, onion, garlic, lemon juice and peel, and fresh thyme if you have it, plus the spices that have previously steeped.

3. Stir until the sugar and salt are dissolved, then submerge the chicken(s) entirely in the brine (see notes). Cover and refrigerate for several hours or preferably overnight.

4. Pull the chicken from the brine and pat the skin dry with paper towels. Rub the entire surface of the chicken with the olive oil.

5. Season the skin with a little chopped fresh thyme.

6. Boil 1 lemon in water for about 10 minutes.

note > The brine amount is sufficient for 2 chickens if the container is the right size. The container should be big enough to be able to hold the chickens plus the brining liquid and have the chickens completely submerged. The same brine works well for turkey too.

note > There's no need to season the chicken with salt before placing it in the oven. Brining the chicken will completely season the meat. If you are not brining the chicken, go ahead and season the chicken with salt.

7.   Stab the lemon about a dozen times with a fork and stuff it into the cavity of the bird along with the thyme and garlic cloves.

8.   Roast uncovered on a rack in a preheated 375°F oven until a meat thermometer reaches 185°F when inserted into the thickest part of the breast meat (approximate 1½ hours or longer, depending on the weight of the chicken).

9.   Allow the chicken to rest for 10-15 minutes before carving. Cut the lemon in half and squeeze the juice onto the carved chicken pieces before serving.

Takeout Orange Chicken

PREP TIME **15 MINUTES** | COOK TIME **15 MINUTES** | SERVES **6**

FOR THE CHICKEN

4 large boneless, skinless chicken breasts (or 8 boneless, skinless, well-trimmed chicken thighs)

salt and pepper to season

1 cup flour

1 tsp black pepper

1 tsp fine salt

1 tsp five-spice powder

1 tsp powdered ginger

1 egg + 2 tbsp water

a few tbsp of peanut oil or canola oil

FOR THE SAUCE

1 tbsp peanut oil or canola oil

3 cloves garlic, minced

1¼ cups frozen orange juice concentrate, approximately (I use a 295ml container)

½ cup water

⅓ cup honey

¼ cup rice wine vinegar

1 tbsp ginger root, freshly grated

2 tsp crushed chili paste, or chili flakes to taste

2 tbsp light soy sauce

2 tsp toasted sesame oil

1 tsp Chinese five-spice powder

2 tbsp cornstarch dissolved in ¼ cup water

Quick, easy, and baked, not fried. A very flavourful version of a Chinese-style takeout dish that uses economical frozen orange juice concentrate as the base of the tangy sauce.

Skip ordering in and make this simple, amazing homemade dish in no time. No need for weekly takeout when you have flavourful dishes like this in your recipe arsenal.

TO MAKE THE CHICKEN

1. Heat a cookie sheet in the oven at 425°F. This speeds up the cooking time later.

2. Cut the chicken into 2-bite pieces and season them lightly with salt and pepper.

3. Sift together the flour, pepper, salt, five-spice powder, and powdered ginger.

4. Whisk together the egg and water to make an egg wash.

5. Dredge the chicken pieces into the flour mixture to coat them, then dip the pieces in the egg wash and back into the flour and spice dredge again.

6. Working quickly, retrieve the cookie sheet from the oven and lightly brush the entire bottom with the oil. Add the coated chicken pieces to the sheet but don't crowd them together; they should not be touching. Lightly drizzle a little more oil over the chicken pieces. A spray bottle works well for this.

7. Pop the chicken into the oven for 8 minutes. Take the sheet out and turn the chicken pieces over before putting them back into the oven for another 7-8 minutes. Cut one open to see that they are fully cooked. This should be plenty of time at that temperature.

tip > We most often serve steamed vegetables on the side with this dish, but if you like, you can also toss in red peppers, cooked green beans or snow peas, water chestnuts, or steamed broccoli with the chicken when adding the sauce. Use any combination of vegetables you like to make this a complete meal.

8. Toss the cooked chicken pieces with the sauce and serve over steamed rice or Chinese noodles.

9. Garnish with toasted sesame seeds and chopped green onions, if you like.

TO MAKE THE SAUCE

1. In a small saucepan over medium heat, quickly sauté the garlic in the peanut oil for only a minute or so.

2. Add all of the remaining ingredients to the pot, except the cornstarch and water.

3. Bring the sauce to a slow simmer for 5 minutes.

4. Stir the cornstarch into the water and add it to the sauce, stirring constantly. Simmer for only 1 more minute, stirring constantly.

Drumstick Stew *with* Summer Savoury Gravy and Dumplings, a.k.a. Doughboys

PREP TIME **30 MINUTES** | COOK TIME **2 HOURS** | SERVES **6**

2 tbsp olive oil or butter

2 red onions, finely diced

4 cloves garlic, minced

salt and pepper to season

3 lbs chicken drumsticks, skinned (see note below before throwing out skins)

4 cups (1 litre) low sodium chicken stock

2 lbs red or yellow potatoes, cut in 2-inch chunks

4 large carrots, cut in coins

2 large parsnips, cut in coins (optional)

1 cup frozen peas

3 tbsp summer savoury (Mt. Scio Farms Brand is best)

3 bay leaves

1 tsp poultry seasoning, or ½ tsp powdered sage

½ tsp black pepper or to taste (I like a peppery stew)

4 tbsp flour mixed with ½ cup cold water, as a thickening slurry

This stew is an economical, flavourful, and satisfying comfort food meal, made with staple ingredients and affordable chicken drumsticks. You can also add dumplings if you like, known here in Newfoundland as doughboys. For generations they have been an economical way to stretch a hearty comfort food meal further.

1. Preheat oven to 325°F. Place the olive oil or butter in a large Dutch oven on the stovetop over medium heat.

2. Add the onions and garlic, lightly season with salt and pepper, and cook just until the onions begin to soften.

3. Place the skinned drumsticks on top of the onion and garlic and lightly season the top again.

4. Place the lid on the Dutch oven and place in the preheated oven for about 1 hour and 15 minutes.

5. Remove from the oven and add the chicken stock, all of the vegetables, savoury, bay leaves, poultry seasoning, and black pepper. Season with a little more salt if necessary. (If adding the finely chopped crispy chicken skin, add it now. See tip below.)

> **tip** > In this recipe I've even used the chicken skin to enhance the flavour of the gravy. The drumsticks are braised without their skins to cut the fat in the meal, but I don't throw out those skins. I lay them out flat on a cookie sheet lined with parchment paper and bake them in a 350°F oven for about 20-25 minutes or until they are golden brown and very crispy, like crisp cooked bacon. All of the fat renders out of the skins, which I blot with paper towels to remove any surface fat. I then chop them into fine crumbs of crispy chicken skin, which I add to the pot when adding the vegetables. The result is like adding a natural bouillon cube without the added salt. It really amps up the flavour in any gravy you are making.

6. Return to the oven for 45 minutes or until the vegetables are fork tender.

7. Remove the chicken legs from the stew and strip all of the meat from the bones.

8. Bring the stew to a slow simmer on top of the stove.

9. Mix the flour and water together so that there are no lumps.

10. Slowly add to the simmering stew, stirring constantly.

11. Add the chicken back to the pot and simmer for only a couple of minutes before serving. (If you are adding dumplings, you will be putting the stew back into the oven.)

TO MAKE THE DOUGHBOYS

1. Sift together the flour, sugar, baking powder, baking soda, and salt.

2. Using a wooden spoon, very quickly mix in the warm milk and melted butter. Do not overwork this dough. Stir in the liquid as quickly as possible and as soon as a soft dough forms, stop mixing.

3. Give the stew one last good stir to make sure that nothing is sticking to the bottom of the pot, then drop the dough by heaping tablespoonfuls into the slowly simmering stew.

4. Place the cover on the pot and pop it back in the oven for another 15 minutes. It's important not to remove the lid during this time so the doughboys cook properly.

5. Remove the doughboys from the pot and give the stew a final stir before serving.

FOR THE DOUGHBOYS
OPTIONAL, MAKES ABOUT 10

2 cups flour

2 tbsp sugar

2 tsp baking powder

1 tsp baking soda

½ tsp salt

1 cup warm milk

¼ cup melted butter

Curry Chicken Salad
with Apricots and Walnuts

PREP TIME **15 MINUTES** | COOK TIME **10 MINUTES** | SERVES **4**

If you're looking for something to do with that leftover chicken in the fridge, this is a bright, intensely flavourful twist on good ol' chicken salad. The dried fruit and nuts add great texture.

Serve on some crusty bread as sandwiches, or atop a green salad for a complete meal. I've even served this chicken salad between slices of baguette cut into mini sandwiches as party finger food, and guests raved about them.

¼ cup walnuts

2 cups leftover cooked chicken

¼ cup dried apricots, chopped

¼ cup low fat mayo

¼ cup red bell pepper, diced finely

1 tbsp apple cider vinegar

1 tbsp chives, chopped, or 2 tbsp green onion

1 tbsp honey

½ tsp yellow curry powder

salt and pepper to taste

1. Place walnuts on a small cookie tray and bake for 10 minutes at 350°F. Toss the walnuts at the halfway point to help them toast evenly.

2. Let the nuts cool for 10-15 minutes, then roughly chop them.

3. Toss all of the ingredients together until well combined. Add a little more mayo if the dressing seems to be too thin.

Honey Garlic Barbecue Chicken

PREP TIME **20 MINUTES** | COOK TIME **40 MINUTES** | SERVES **6**

This is a recent addition to *RockRecipes.com* and one that was an instant hit. On tasting it for the first time, I just knew I would have to add it to this cookbook.

Using a lower fat, oven-baked method makes this recipe an easy but utterly delicious chicken dinner.

The chicken is seasoned with our Smokin' Summer Spice Dry Rub (page 12) before being dredged, baked, and finished with a sweet and sticky honey garlic barbecue sauce. Serve it and people will ask for the recipe. Guaranteed.

FOR THE CHICKEN

3   tbsp canola oil

2-3 lbs boneless, skinless chicken thighs or breasts (see notes below for using breasts)

4   tbsp Smokin' Summer Spice Dry Rub (page 12), or BBQ seasoning (approximately)

1   cup flour (approximately)

FOR THE SAUCE

2   tbsp olive oil

4   cloves garlic, minced

½   cup honey

1   cup BBQ Sauce

½   tsp chili flakes (optional)

½   tsp black pepper

pinch salt

TO MAKE THE CHICKEN

1. Preheat the oven to 400°F.

2. Line a baking sheet with parchment paper and brush the canola oil over the parchment paper.

3. Lay the boneless skinless breasts flat on a cutting board and liberally season with the spice rub on both sides.

4. Fold them in half and dredge in the flour until completely coated. (They should remain folded while dredging in the flour.)

5. Bake for about 45 minutes, turning the chicken pieces over at the 20-minute mark, until they reach 170°F when tested with a meat thermometer. Check earlier than the 45-minute mark if the pieces are small. They may well be fully cooked before that time.

notes >

If using boneless, skinless chicken breasts, pound them out to a uniform thickness or butterfly cut them to make them flatter. You can then fold them in half before dredging in the flour, so that they will be seasoned inside and out, the same as thighs would be.

Chicken breasts may cook faster than chicken thighs, depending on their thickness. Use a meat thermometer to determine whether chicken is fully cooked. It's done when it reaches 170°F.

TO MAKE THE SAUCE

1. Add the olive oil and garlic to a small saucepan.

2. Cook over medium-low heat for about 1 minute, until the garlic just softens but does not brown.

3. Add the honey and let it come to a slow simmer for a few minutes.

4. Add the BBQ sauce, chili flakes if using them, plus the pepper and salt.

5. Simmer slowly for 5 minutes or so, stirring often.

6. Dip the cooked chicken pieces in the sauce and serve.

Chicken Tikka Masala

PREP TIME 30 MINUTES | **COOK TIME 50 MINUTES** | **SERVES 8**

FOR THE CHICKEN

3 lbs boneless, skinless chicken thighs or breasts

FOR THE MARINADE

¾ cup plain yogurt

¼ cup tomato juice, drained from the diced tomatoes used in the sauce later

2 cloves garlic, minced

2 tbsp fresh ginger, roughly grated

2 tsp tandoori masala, or 1 tbsp chili powder

1 tsp garam masala

1 tsp paprika

½ tsp black pepper, coarsely ground

½ tsp crushed chili paste, or about 1 tsp chili flakes

½ tsp salt

FOR THE MARINADE

1 tbsp garam masala

1 tbsp smoked paprika

1 tsp cumin

1 tsp turmeric

1 tsp yellow curry powder

½ tsp cloves

½ tsp ground cardamom

½ tsp ground coriander seed

2 tbsp peanut oil, or other vegetable oil

2 medium-sized onions, diced

2 cloves garlic, minced

one 28-oz can diced tomatoes

1 cup chicken stock

1 tbsp honey

½ cup whipping cream (optional) or add ¾ cup yogurt

Here's a curry classic the easy way. Make this flavour-packed, classic curry dish easily and economically, even as a low-fat version. Simple spices and ingredients yield big taste in this family favourite.

I always keep the central spices like garam masala and a couple of curry powders, like red and yellow, on hand, but this is a versatile recipe you can adjust to your tastes.

I always say to make curry the way you like it. Add more or less of any of the spices to suit your taste or heat preference, and make no apologies for it. You know your taste best.

TO MAKE THE CHICKEN

1. Trim the chicken pieces of any excess visible fat. If you're using chicken breasts, cut them into two or three pieces. Thighs, I usually leave whole. The chicken will be cut into smaller pieces later anyway.

2. Mix all of the ingredients in the marinade together and add the chicken. You can do this in a large zip-lock bag or in a covered glass bowl. Make sure all of the chicken pieces are well coated. Leave to marinate in the fridge for anywhere from a couple of hours to overnight.

3. Do not scrape off the marinade before cooking the chicken on a gas grill, a hot cast iron grill pan, or on a rack about 6 inches from your broiler. The chicken should get good char marks on the grill or grill pan or a speckle of char under the broiler. Turned once, my chicken thighs took about 20 minutes under the broiler.

4. Set the cooked chicken aside to rest for a few minutes, then cut it into bite-sized pieces and add it to the tikka masala sauce.

TO MAKE THE SAUCE

1. Mix together the garam masala, smoked paprika, cumin, turmeric, yellow curry powder, cloves, cardamom, and coriander seed. Set aside to add later.

2. In a small Dutch oven, heat the oil over medium heat. Add the onions and garlic and cook until the onions soften and just begin to turn golden.

3. Add the spices you mixed earlier and let them heat up for a minute or so as you toss them with the cooked onions.

4. Add the diced tomatoes, chicken stock, and honey.

5. Simmer slowly for 20 minutes then add the chicken pieces and simmer for an additional 10 minutes. If using cream or yogurt in the sauce, add it with the chicken.

6. Serve over plain steamed rice or with warm naan.

Panko Chicken Caesar Burgers

PREP TIME 15 MINUTES | COOK TIME 15 MINUTES | SERVES 4

Easy crispy fried panko chicken breasts make the ideal tender and juicy base for these tasty fast-food alternative chicken burgers. In my humble opinion, they are better than any takeout chicken burger I've ever tried.

Use your own favourite Caesar salad dressing if you like, but I recommend trying our very intensely tasty homemade version, featuring the bold sweet flavour of roasted garlic. I predict you'll make that dressing again and again.

4　large boneless, skinless chicken breasts (6 oz each)

½　cup plain flour

1　egg + 2 tbsp water, whisked together to make an egg wash

1 cup panko

canola oil for frying

¾　cup part skim mozzarella cheese, grated

¼　cup Parmesan cheese, grated

romaine lettuce

Roasted Garlic Caesar Salad Dressing (see Steak Bacon Walnut Blue Cheese Caesar Salad recipe on page 52), or any Caesar dressing you have

8　strips smoked bacon, cooked

4　whole wheat kaiser rolls or hamburger buns, toasted

1. Dip the chicken breasts in flour and then the egg wash, followed by the panko crumbs.

2. Heat half an inch of canola oil in a large skillet over medium-low heat and fry the chicken breasts until golden brown. I like to take the internal temperature of the breasts to make sure they hit 170°F to be certain they are fully cooked. If they are getting too brown, finish them in a 350°F oven until the right temperature is reached.

3. Top with a mixture of the mozza and Parmesan cheeses and place under the broiler for 1 minute to melt the cheese. Toss the romaine lettuce with a little Caesar dressing and serve along with the chicken and cooked bacon on toasted kaiser rolls.

> **tip** > To get the chicken cooking quickly, remove it from the fridge about 30 minutes before the cooking time, still in the package or well covered in plastic wrap, and let it come closer to room temperature. Using the chicken breasts straight from the fridge lengthens the time for the heat to get to the centre of the meat. This tip applies equally to the shallow-fried and oven-baked versions of this recipe.

for a lower fat, baked version, use the oven method >

1. Preheat a cookie sheet in the oven at 425°F. This preheating helps to get the chicken started cooking as soon as possible.

2. Prepare and coat your chicken breasts exactly the same way as directed in the shallow-fried version of the recipe.

3. When the chicken is ready to go in the oven, cover the hot cookie sheet in parchment paper and brush a little canola oil over the surface of the paper.

4. Place the coated breasts on the prepared sheet and drizzle lightly with a couple of teaspoons of oil. An oil spray bottle will allow you to use as little as possible while still getting a very even coating of oil on the surface. It really doesn't take much oil at all to get the oven-baked breasts crispy.

5. After 10 minutes in the oven, flip the chicken and bake for another 10 minutes. Take an internal temperature reading, to make sure they reach about 170°F on a meat thermometer. If not, flip them again and return to the oven for another 5 minutes and test them again. Repeat if necessary, but in all likelihood only quite thick breasts would need more time.

Chicken Chili Rice and Beans

PREP TIME **10 MINUTES** | COOK TIME **30 MINUTES** | SERVES **6**

With everyone feeling the pinch of high food prices these days, delicious and economical meals like rice and beans are a welcome addition to any weekly meal plan. Here's one of our family's go-to dinners that uses less expensive chicken thighs and a few pantry and freezer staples to create a delicious comfort food dinner.

Nutritious without sacrificing any flavour, this recipe feeds up to six for under $15. Who doesn't need more recipe ideas like that?

2	tbsp canola oil
1½-2	lbs boneless, skinless chicken thighs or breasts, well-trimmed of visible fat and diced into bite-sized pieces

salt and pepper to season

1	large onion, diced fine
3	cloves garlic, minced
3½	cups canned diced tomatoes
2½	cups canned kidney beans, well rinsed (I use a 600ml can)
2	tbsp chili powder or more to taste
½	tsp ground cumin

salt and pepper to season

2	cups frozen corn, thawed
6	cups steamed rice

1. In a Dutch oven, heat the canola oil over medium heat and add the diced chicken. Season with salt and pepper and cook until the chicken has lightly browned.

2. Remove the chicken from the pot and set aside.

3. Add the onions and garlic to the pot and cook until the onions begin to soften.

4. Add the tomatoes, kidney beans, chili powder, and cumin. Season with salt and pepper and simmer for 15 minutes.

5. Add the browned chicken back to the pot along with the thawed corn and bring back to a simmer for an additional 15 minutes before serving over the steamed rice.

Taco Wings *with* Spicy Guacamole Dip

PREP TIME **25** MINUTES | COOK TIME **10** MINUTES | SERVES **10**

canola or peanut oil for deep frying

2 lbs **chicken wings,** washed and trimmed

FOR THE HERB AND SPICE DREDGE

2 cups flour

2 tbsp **chili powder** (the kind you would use making chili con carne)

1 tbsp **dried oregano,** or Mexican oregano

1 tbsp **ground ginger**

1 tbsp **smoked paprika,** or regular paprika

2 tsp **fine salt**

1 tsp **cinnamon**

1 tsp **cumin**

1 tsp **black pepper,** freshly ground

½ tsp **cayenne pepper,** or more or less to your heat preference (optional)

FOR THE SPICY GUACAMOLE DIP

2 cups **avocado,** mashed

½ cup **sour cream**

2 cloves **garlic,** finely minced

1 tsp **crushed chili paste**

salt and **pepper** to season

When it comes to party food, we are no slouches in this household. We have hosted many great social gatherings over the years and always try to keep things new and interesting when serving our guests.

We are especially known for our many versions of chicken wings, which we serve at get-togethers with friends. We now have dozens of them on *RockRecipes.com*.

This recipe is an exciting infusion of bright Mexican flavours and colours, making these wings perfect for Cinco de Mayo, game days, or any time you come together with friends and family for a celebration!

---

1. Add canola oil or peanut oil to your deep fryer and preheat to 350°F.

2. Dredge the chicken wings into the flour and spice mixture.

3. Dip each wing quickly in the egg wash and then back into the flour and spice mixture. This double-dipped method helps keep the crust on the wings and makes them super crispy too.

4. Repeat for all the wings. Lay them on a cutting board while the oil heats.

5. Fry for about 8-12 minutes, depending upon the size of the wings, until medium golden brown and a meat thermometer reaches 170°F.

6. Drain on a wire rack placed on a cookie sheet.

7. Hold in a 175°F oven if making more than one batch. Serve with Spicy Guacamole Dip.

TO MAKE THE SAUCE

1. Simply mash and mix ingredients to combine, or give it a minute in the food processor.

2. Cover with plastic wrap and chill until ready to serve.

The Best Fried Chicken

PREP TIME **20 MINUTES** | COOK TIME **20 MINUTES** | SERVES **4-6**

3-4 lbs fresh chicken pieces

2 cups buttermilk or whole milk

vegetable oil for deep frying

FOR THE CHICKEN BRINE

2 litres water

¼ cup brown sugar

¼ cup kosher salt

1 tbsp dried thyme

1 tbsp peppercorns

2 cloves garlic, chopped

2 bay leaves

FOR THE COATING/DREDGE

2 cups flour

2 tbsp onion powder

1 tbsp dried basil

1 tbsp dried marjoram

1 tbsp dried oregano

1 tbsp dry mustard powder

1 tbsp garlic powder

1 tbsp ground black pepper

1 tbsp paprika

1 tbsp powdered ginger

1 tbsp powdered sage

1 tbsp powdered thyme

1 tbsp salt

1 tsp cayenne pepper

Another family favourite at our house that my son liked to refer to as DFC or Daddy Fried Chicken. I use twelve herbs and spices, and I do like to brine my chicken before frying, but this stage is optional. You will find that your chicken is moister, better seasoned, and more flavourful if brined.

Regardless, serve this chicken with some buttermilk biscuits, mashed potatoes, and sweet corn, and you've got yourself a delicious and authentic Southern meal.

---

1. Cut a whole large chicken (about 3-4 lbs) into pieces and trim them well, or just use 4 lbs of well-trimmed chicken pieces. I like to remove the backbone from the thigh portions in particular to get quicker and more even cooking.

2. For the brine (optional), mix together all the ingredients until the salt and sugar is dissolved.

3. Soak the trimmed chicken pieces in the brine for up to 24 hours in the refrigerator.

4. Remove the chicken pieces from brine, rinse pieces well in cold water, and pat dry. Let the pieces air-dry for 30 minutes, which will also allow the chicken to come up to room temperature before frying. This is very helpful in maintaining a consistent temperature in the fryer.

5. Combine all of the ingredients for the coating and mix thoroughly to make sure spices are evenly distributed in the mix.

6. Fill your deep fryer to the appropriate level with vegetable oil. Canola or peanut oil is good. Preheat the deep fryer to 350°F.

7. Dunk the chicken pieces into the buttermilk and let the excess drip off.

tip > The coating mix in this recipe is enough to do about three batches of chicken. Make less of the flour dredge mix if you like or just separate it into three portions and store the other two portions in zip-lock bags or an airtight container until the next time you need it.

8. Dredge chicken pieces in the coating. I like to cover each piece with the coating mix and then give it a good press down to make sure all of the chicken comes into good contact with the flour dredge.

note > Some people like to double dip their chicken for a thicker, crunchier crust, returning the pieces to the buttermilk and then the flour and spice mix for a second time. You can do so if you wish.

9. Place chicken pieces on a plate and allow to sit for 10 minutes before frying.

10. Drop chicken pieces into hot oil, starting with the largest pieces first. Try and maintain the oil at 350°F throughout the cooking time. Do not crowd your fryer. Four or five large pieces or five or six small pieces at a time is enough. Large pieces can take about 20 minutes to cook, smaller pieces 15-20 minutes. I always use my meat thermometer as a guide to get the internal temperature of the chicken pieces to a safe 170°F.

note > My fryer can only take 4 or 5 pieces at a time, so hold the cooked pieces in a 175°F oven while the other pieces fry.

11. Remove cooked chicken to a wire rack to cool slightly before serving.

With so many people cutting back on red meat in recent years, I now tend to look at it as a celebration ingredient. The beef recipes here reflect that view in delicious ideas from an amazing prime rib roast dinner to my version of a classic Philly cheesesteak sandwich.

I've often said that I think pork is both the most versatile and, too often, the most underused protein. Lean cuts of pork can be as low in fat as chicken, while others like crowd favourite pork belly, should also fall into the celebration ingredient category.

This time around we've got taste bud-tempting suggestions from homestyle comfort food classics like pork stew to my quick and easy take on a Cubano sandwich in burger form. These are recipes that will take you from weekday dinners to weekend dinner parties with ease.

beef & pork

Asian Glazed Pork Belly

PREP TIME **10 MINUTES** | COOK TIME **HOURS** | SERVES **8 OR MORE**

Pork belly is an incredibly flavourful and versatile cut of meat. I particularly love it in this recipe with a fusion of Asian flavours. The secret is low and slow cooking to render the fat and achieve that perfect, rich, soft, silky, tender texture. The perfectly cooked pork belly doesn't feel like you are biting into a chunk of bland fat, like some I've sampled, even in restaurants.

This recipe is a little sweet, a little sticky, a little salty, a little spicy, and so deliciously satisfying.

note > It is important to get a piece of pork belly that is a uniform thickness so that it cooks evenly. Try to get a piece that is about 3 inches thick. If thinner pieces are all that is available, I usually stack them and tie them with pieces of butcher string after the meat has marinated.

3	lbs pork belly (approximately)
¼	cup hoisin sauce
¼	cup honey
¼	cup low sodium soy sauce
2	tbsp rice vinegar
1	tbsp fish sauce
1	tbsp fresh ginger, grated
2	tsp chili flakes
1½	tsp Chinese five-spice powder
1	tsp black pepper

1. Mix all of the ingredients in the marinade together and pour over the pork belly in a large zip-lock bag.

2. Marinate in the fridge for several hours or overnight.

3. Preheat the oven to 275°F.

4. Place the pork belly on a roasting rack and roast for 4-5 hours depending upon the thickness of the meat.

5. Reserve the marinade and pour it into your smallest saucepan. You can add all the same ingredients again to make extra sauce/glaze for rice or noodles at this point if you like.

6. Slowly simmer the marinade until it begins to become like a thin syrup, about maple syrup consistency.

7. In the last couple of hours of roasting, begin to brush on layers of the glaze. I do this 4-6 times about every 20 minutes, to build good, flavourful, sticky glaze on the pork belly.

8. Let the pork belly rest for about 15 minutes before slicing and serving. I also like to dice it into small bite-sized chunks to serve over rice.

tip > I like to trim the outermost layer of rind/ skin off of pork belly, especially when slowly oven roasting, because it can become quite tough. It is also best to roast with the fattiest side up.

Balsamic Braised Beef

PREP TIME **15 MINUTES** | COOK TIME **2 HOURS 30 MINUTES** | SERVES **6 OR MORE**

This is a little different but still a great slow-cooked Sunday dinner. The beef roast is sealed inside aluminum foil and braised slowly in its own juices, plus a very flavourful but simple jus.

The meat is tender and moist. The jus is well balanced with sharp and slightly sweet flavours combining with the hearty flavour of the beef. This meal is perfectly paired with some good ol' mashed potatoes.

3 lb cross rib roast	
3 tbsp canola oil	
4 tbsp Worcestershire sauce	
2 tbsp balsamic vinegar	
2 tbsp bold deli mustard or English mustard	
2 tsp honey or molasses	
1 tsp dried thyme	
½ tsp nutmeg	
½ tsp black pepper	
½ tsp salt	
3 tbsp butter	
3 cloves garlic, minced	

1.   Heat the canola oil in a cast iron pan over medium-high heat.

2.   Season the beef roast with salt and pepper and brown the roast well on all sides.

3.   Transfer the beef roast to a covered roasting pan that has been lined with wide-roll, heavy-duty aluminum foil, plus enough to fold over as a cover for the beef.

4.   Stir together the Worcestershire sauce, balsamic vinegar, mustard, honey, thyme, nutmeg, pepper, and salt. Set aside.

5.   Let the pan cool for a couple of minutes, then drain the excess fat off the pan and add the butter and garlic over medium-low heat for just a minute until the garlic slightly softens.

6.   Remove from heat and add all of the remaining ingredients that have been stirred together.

7.   Scrape the bottom of the pan to release any sticky bits left behind. Pour the contents of the pan onto the beef roast.

8.   Roll the edges of the heavy-duty aluminum foil to completely seal the roast inside, then add the cover to the roasting pan.

9.   Roast at 300°F for about 3 hours or until the roast is fall-apart tender.

FOR THE TOMATO SAUCE

2 tbsp olive oil

4 cloves garlic, minced

1 small red onion, finely diced

6 cups canned San Marzano tomatoes, pureed (I mostly buy whole or chopped canned tomatoes and puree them myself in the food processor or blender)

4 tbsp balsamic vinegar

2 tbsp brown sugar

1 tsp black pepper, freshly ground

1 tsp dried oregano leaves

1 tsp kosher salt

pinch chili flakes, or to taste

FOR THE MEATBALLS

1½ cups bread crumbs, lightly packed

½ cup milk

1½ lbs ground beef

1½ lbs ground pork

2 eggs

½ cup Parmesan cheese, finely grated

4 cloves garlic, finely minced

2 tbsp fresh Italian parsley, chopped

1½ tsp ground fennel seeds (I crush them with a mortar and pestle, but you can crush them in a sandwich bag using a mallet or hammer if you can't find pre-ground.)

1 tsp black pepper, freshly ground

1 tsp dried oregano

1 tsp kosher salt

1 tsp paprika, or smoked paprika

½ tsp chili flakes, or to taste

YOU WILL ALSO NEED

About 1 pound of dry spaghetti pasta, cooked to al dente in plenty of salted boiling water. Drain but do not rinse the pasta before serving

Best Spaghetti and Meatballs

PREP TIME **45 MINUTES**

COOK TIME **40 MINUTES** | SERVES **8**

Spaghetti and meatballs is a real icon of comfort food dishes. It's the kind of good, old-fashioned, hearty meal that I grew up on and still love.

My version mixes both beef and pork and echoes the flavours of good Italian sausage in the tender, juicy meatballs. I like to keep the tomato sauce as simple as possible too.

You really can't go wrong with this approach, which always produces a flavourful family favourite.

TO MAKE THE SAUCE

1. Prepare the sauce first so that it can simmer and reduce while you prepare the meatballs.

2. In a Dutch oven, heat the olive oil over medium heat. Add the garlic and onions and sauté together until the onions have softened but not browned.

3. Add all of the remaining ingredients for the sauce and simmer on low heat while you prepare the meatballs.

TO MAKE THE MEATBALLS

1. Pour the milk over the bread crumbs and let them soak while you gather the other ingredients in the meatball recipe.

2. Put all ingredients in a large bowl and mix together well.

3. Form into balls 2½ inches in diameter. Keeping your hands wet with cold water prevents the mixture from sticking to your hands.

4. Brown the meatballs on all sides in a non-stick frying pan for about 10 minutes. You want to get some good colour on them.

5. Add the meatballs to the simmering sauce in the Dutch oven.

6. Simmer slowly for about 30 minutes before serving over al dente cooked spaghetti with a garnish of additional Parmesan cheese.

Pork Stew *with* Sage and Thyme

PREP TIME **30 MINUTES** | COOK TIME **2 HOURS** | SERVES **6 OR MORE**

Like my other stews, this recipe is a satisfying and economical dish. Making sure your meat is well browned is probably the most important step in starting to build layers of flavour to produce a rich, savory stew.

This is a good old-fashioned, stick to your ribs recipe when you're looking for a comfort food meal. It's excellent served with dumplings, cornbread, or biscuits too.

---

3 tbsp olive oil

3 cloves garlic, minced

1 large white onion

3 lbs pork shoulder or sirloin, cut in about 1-inch cubes

pinch salt and pepper to season

3 stalks celery, chopped

4 tbsp fresh sage, chopped

2 tbsp fresh thyme leaves

5 cups total of pork stock, divided into 2 cups + 3 cups (vegetable stock or chicken stock works too)

4 carrots, sliced into coins

6 large potatoes, cut into 1½-inch cubes

½ cup water

4 rounded tbsp flour

1 cup corn kernels, fresh or frozen

1 cup peas, fresh or frozen

1. Begin by bringing the stock to a slow simmer and keep it on low heat until needed. This will help speed up the cooking time.

2. Over medium-high heat add the olive oil to the bottom of a heavy-bottom Dutch oven.

3. Add the onions and garlic and cook until soft and partly caramelized. Remove from the pot and set aside.

note > You may or may not need to add another tbsp of olive oil at this point.

4. Add the pork to the heated pan, season with salt and pepper, and cook for about 5 minutes, tossing often until the pork is well browned.

5. To the hot pot, add the celery and caramelized onions and garlic.

6. Add the sage and thyme plus 2 cups of the pork stock. The stock should be boiling hot to speed up the cooking time of this recipe.

7. Stir together, cover, and place in a 350°F oven for about 1 hour.

8. Taste the broth and add more salt and pepper as needed. I like a peppery stew.

tip > A nice finishing touch is to stir in some extra chopped fresh thyme and sage while thickening the stew. It gives the stew a little fresh boost of flavour.

9. After the hour, add the carrots with the remaining 3 cups of boiling hot stock.

10. Return to the oven for 20 minutes then add the potatoes.

11. Return to the oven for another 20-30 minutes until the potatoes are fork tender.

12. Move the stew to the stovetop and bring to a gentle boil over medium heat.

13. Make a thickening slurry by whisking together the flour and water until no lumps are left. Slowly add the slurry, stirring constantly to avoid lumps.

14. Add the corn and peas to the pot.

15. Simmer for 1 or 2 minutes and serve.

Philly Cheesesteak

PREP TIME **25 MINUTES** | COOK TIME **30 MINUTES** | SERVES **6 SIX-INCH SANDWICH ROLLS**

Everything you ever read about Philly cheesesteak sandwiches says that the only real cheesesteaks are to be found in Philadelphia itself. I'm not going to argue with that. I've only ever eaten one Philly cheesesteak in Philadelphia, on my only visit to the city. It was at Campo's Deli on Market Street, and it was definitely the best I've had anywhere.

This recipe is a near-perfect version of this famous sandwich that you can make at home, on the closest thing to an authentic cheesesteak roll I've ever tried.

FOR THE ROLLS

1⅓ cups water, lukewarm

4 tsp sugar

1 envelope active dry yeast, 7-8 grams or about 2 tsp, not instant yeast

3 cups all-purpose flour + a little more for kneading

1½ tsp salt

2 tbsp olive oil, plus a little more to brush on the rolls

FOR THE CHEESESTEAK FILLING

2 lbs rib-eye beef, or strip loin, thinly sliced

salt and pepper to season

a little canola oil

a little Worcestershire sauce (optional)

sliced provolone cheese

TO MAKE THE ROLLS

1. In a small bowl or measuring cup, dissolve 1 tsp sugar in ⅓ cup of the lukewarm water

2. Sprinkle the yeast over the water and let stand for 10-15 minutes until the yeast activates and becomes foamy.

3. Meanwhile combine the flour, 3 tsp sugar, and salt in the bowl of a stand mixer with the dough hook attached.

4. Add the proofed yeast and the remaining 1 cup lukewarm water.

5. Mix on low speed until the dough has been kneaded for at least 5 minutes before adding the olive oil and letting it work its way into the dough.

6. Turn the dough out onto a very lightly floured bread board or countertop.

notes >

Be careful not to add a lot of flour in the kneading process. You still want the dough to be a little bit sticky right through to the end stages. This ensures that the final inside texture of the roll is soft with the gluten well developed and not a denser texture with tight bubbles.

Knead the dough by hand for 5 minutes, even after it comes out of the stand mixer, remembering to use as little flour as possible. Use the heel of your hand to stretch the dough across the kneading surface in a sort of smearing action, then fold the dough back over itself, turn it around and do the same again. Keep repeating this action for at least five minutes to develop good gluten in the dough.

7. Knead the dough by hand for at least 5 minutes after it comes out of the stand mixer, remembering to use as little flour as possible.

8. Use the heel of your hand to stretch the dough across the kneading surface in a sort of smearing action, then fold the dough back over itself, turn it around a half turn, and do the same again. Keep repeating this action for at least 5-10 minutes to develop good gluten in the dough. The dough should appear relatively smooth but still a little sticky to the touch.

9. Lightly oil a large bowl with olive oil, place the dough inside, cover it with plastic wrap, and let it sit in a warm place for at least 1 hour until the dough doubles in size.

tip > Never add the olive oil with the rest of the ingredients; this will inhibit production of gluten and form a less elastic dough. Add the oil only after the gluten strands have already begun to form within the dough. (Refer to recipe.)

FORMING THE ROLLS

1. Again on a lightly floured surface, knead the dough back into a ball and cut into 6 equal pieces.

2. Form the dough pieces into about 5-inch lengths and place them a couple of inches apart on a parchment paper-lined cookie sheet. You can dust the parchment with yellow cornmeal if you like, but it shouldn't stick to the parchment paper in any case.

3. Very lightly brush the formed rolls with olive oil. Dust the tops with a little cornmeal too if you like.

4. Drape the cookie sheet loosely with plastic wrap and let the rolls rise in a warm place for at least another hour until they at least double in size. You don't want to rush the dough rising at this stage or else your rolls will be too dense.

5. Preheat the oven to 425°F. The oven MUST be fully preheated. Place a small tray of boiling water in the back corner of the oven. I use an aluminum pie plate. This causes humidity inside the oven, which helps the bread fully rise before forming a crust.

6. Using a very sharp knife or razor blade, quickly but gently cut a ¼-inch deep slit down the centre line of the rolls before immediately popping the tray into the hot oven.

7. Bake for 10 minutes then reduce the heat to 400°F and bake for an additional 20-25 minutes until the rolls are an even golden brown. They should sound hollow when tapped with your finger.

8. Let them cool on a wire rack before serving as fresh as possible with the cooked steak and cheese inside.

CONTINUED ON PAGE 48 >

to make the steak and cheese (I like to prepare them 2 at a time) >

1. Slice the beef as thinly as possible and cut the thin slices into strips. Toss the strips with salt and pepper to season.

2. Heat a large sauté pan on high until it is very hot (a nonstick pan works well) and add just a little canola oil to the pan.

3. Throw half of the beef strips into the hot pan and quickly stir fry, just until the meat loses its red colour. In the final 20 seconds or so, you can throw in a few splashes of Worcestershire sauce to add additional seasoning to the meat (optional).

4. In the pan, divide the beef into 2 portions and quickly arrange it into the approximate size and shape of your rolls. Quickly place the cheese on top of the two meat portions and add the lid of the sauté pan for about 15-20 seconds to melt the cheese.

5. Using a large metal spatula, transfer the meat and melting cheese portions onto a split roll. Serve immediately.

Cuban Sandwich Burgers

PREP TIME **15 MINUTES** | COOK TIME **2 HOURS 30 MINUTES** | SERVES **6 OR MORE**

Cuban sandwiches seem to be everywhere these days. It's a brilliant example of a few simple ingredients coming together to create something fantastic. This burger version is a quicker way to enjoy all the great flavour of a tasty Cuban sandwich.

A simply seasoned ground pork patty gets combined with deli ham, Swiss cheese, and mustard on a crusty burger bun for this ode to the Cuban sandwich. It's differently delicious in burger form.

1   lb coarsely ground pork
1   clove garlic, finely minced
½   tsp dried oregano
¼   tsp ground cumin
salt and pepper to season
4-8 slices Swiss cheese
4   crusty burger buns
yellow mustard
6-8 ounces thinly sliced deli ham
sliced dill pickles

1.   Sprinkle the ground pork with the minced garlic, oregano, and cumin. Knead the seasonings into the ground pork a little so that it holds together better to form into patties.

2.   Form the ground pork into four 5-inch patties. Season well with salt and pepper.

3.   Fry the patties in a non-stick pan until well browned and the internal temperature of the patties is 160-170°F. During the last 1 or 2 minutes of cooking time, add 1 or 2 slices of cheese on top of the patties to melt.

4.   Toast the buns under the broiler and spread yellow mustard on both sides. Place about 1½-2 ounces of deli ham on each bun.

5.   Add the cooked patties with the melted cheese on top of the ham, then add sliced dill pickles before topping with the second half of the bun. Serve immediately.

Pineapple Pork Meatballs

PREP TIME **25 MINUTES** | COOK TIME **50 MINUTES** | SERVES **8** (ABOUT **2** DOZEN MEATBALLS)

FOR THE MEATBALLS

1	cup	bread crumbs, lightly packed
¼	cup	milk
2	lbs	coarsely ground pork
1		egg
4	tbsp	green onion, finely chopped
2		cloves garlic, minced
1	tsp	black pepper
1	tsp	kosher salt
½	tsp	ground cumin
½	tsp	ground dried sage
½	tsp	ground dried thyme

FOR THE SAUCE

1½	cups	pineapple juice (reserve ¼ cup of juice)
½	cup	hoisin sauce (substitute ketchup in a pinch)
¼	cup	rice wine vinegar (white wine vinegar or apple cider vinegar can be substituted)
1	tbsp	ginger root, freshly grated
1	tbsp	soy sauce
1	tsp	chili paste or a pinch of chili flakes, more or less to taste
½	tsp	black pepper, freshly ground
½	tsp	Chinese five-spice powder
2	tbsp	honey, or maple syrup (or to taste, see instructions)
2	tbsp	cornstarch, dissolved in the reserved pineapple juice
½		small red pepper, diced small
1½	cups	pineapple, diced

This recipe is a real '70s and '80s throwback for me. We made a version of this many times when I was growing up. It's another economical comfort-food dinner the whole family will love.

My updated version features simply seasoned, all-pork meatballs in an easy to prepare, sweet and sour pineapple sauce. Delicious served over rice or thin Chinese noodles.

TO MAKE THE MEATBALLS

1. Pour the milk over the bread crumbs to soak while you gather the rest of the ingredients.

2. Put all ingredients in a large bowl and mix together well.

3. Form into 2-inch balls. Keeping your hands wet with cold water prevents the mixture from sticking to your hands.

4. Brown the meatballs on all sides in a non-stick frying pan for about 10 minutes. You want to get some good colour on them.

5. Place the meatballs in a covered casserole dish and pour the sauce over them. Bake in a preheated 350°F oven for 30-40 minutes; the sauce should be bubbling well at this point. Serve over steamed rice or thin Chinese noodles.

TO MAKE THE SAUCE

1. In a small saucepan over medium heat, add the peanut oil and minced garlic. Sauté for only about 20-30 seconds to heat the garlic.

2.   Add all of the remaining ingredients except the pineapple, red pepper, and honey or maple syrup, and simmer slowly for 10-15 minutes.

note > I don't add the honey or maple syrup until this point because I like to taste the sauce for balance before thickening it. The pineapple juice may already have sweetened the sauce enough, and you should take into account the sweetness of the pineapple you will be adding. Some very ripe, golden pineapples will add plenty of sweetness all on their own. If the sauce is overly sweet, you can even add another splash of vinegar to balance the sweet and sour in the sauce. Make your own judgment call at this point.

3.   Thicken the sauce with the cornstarch dissolved in the reserved ¼ cup pineapple juice. Add the pineapple and red pepper just before pouring onto the meatballs into the casserole dish.

Steak Bacon Walnut
Blue Cheese Caesar Salad

PREP TIME **25 MINUTES** | COOK TIME **20 MINUTES** | SERVES **4**

FOR THE ROASTED GARLIC CAESAR SALAD DRESSING

1   cup good quality mayonnaise (you may use low fat if you like)

⅓   cup finely grated Parmesan cheese

1   small head of roasted garlic, mashed (see note)

2   tbsp fresh parsley, chopped

2   tbsp of red wine vinegar (or white wine vinegar)

1   tbsp Dijon mustard

1   tbsp Worcestershire sauce

juice of ½ lemon

½   tsp anchovy paste (optional or to taste)

pinch salt and pepper to season

FOR THE SALAD

1   lb thinly sliced steak

¾   cup walnuts, lightly toasted

6 strips bacon, cooked crisp, chopped

1   head romaine lettuce

¾   cup Roasted Garlic Caesar Salad Dressing

¾   cup blue cheese, crumbled

This incredibly flavourful dinner salad was a happy accident waiting to happen. It is a bit of a "fridge cleaner" recipe idea that incorporates a few of my favourite things.

I like to mix it up by switching up the veggies that are the freshest available at the time and using different cheeses, like smoked cheddar.

Substitute your own favourite ingredients for a bold collision of flavours and textures in an outstanding dinner salad that's a complete meal in itself.

---

note > Total preparation time does not include the time to roast the garlic for the dressing.

TO MAKE THE ROASTED GARLIC CAESAR SALAD DRESSING

1.   Mix all of the ingredients together well. You can do this just with a whisk or in a blender or food processor.

2.   Chill well before serving.

TO MAKE THE SALAD

1.   Preheat the oven to 350°F.

2.   Spread the walnuts on a baking tray and bake for about 8 minutes, tossing them halfway through. Set them aside to cool

3.   Slice the steak thinly and chop the cooked bacon.

4.   Wash and dry the lettuce leaves and tear or cut them into bite-sized pieces.

5.   Toss the lettuce with the salad dressing (use more or less dressing to taste) and share evenly between 4 dinner plates.

6.   Evenly scatter the bacon, walnuts, and blue cheese over the dressed lettuce then top each with a portion of sliced steak and serve.

to roast a head of garlic >

Cut a little off the top of the head (¼ inch or so) to reveal the cloves inside. Place the garlic head on a square of aluminum foil, sprinkle on a little salt and pepper to season, and then drizzle with a teaspoon of olive oil. Bring all sides of the aluminum foil together and twist to seal the garlic head inside. Roast in a 350°F oven for about 45 minutes. Squeeze the garlic cloves out of their skins and mash with a fork until a smooth paste forms.

BBQ Prime Rib Steak
with Garlic Chili Butter

PREP TIME **25 MINUTES** | COOK TIME **2 HOURS** | SERVES **8 OR MORE**

This is not an everyday meal, but when I see prime rib roast or steak on sale, I take full advantage. This is a great way to serve it family style.

A dry spice-rubbed prime rib roast gets seared, then slow cooked to succulent perfection. The beef is always the star of the show at a decadent meal like this, but the supporting cast includes an indulgent, flavour-infused butter that really takes it to another level.

Why not take the indulgence factor up on a great cut of meat at your next special occasion or celebration meal?

FOR THE ROAST

3   lbs prime rib roast

salt and pepper to season

Smokin' Summer Spice
Dry Rub (page 12)

FOR THE GARLIC CHILI BUTTER

1   cup + ¼ cup
    softened butter

2-3 cloves garlic, minced

2   tsp chili paste (or 1-2
    small red Thai chilis, finely
    minced)

1   tsp fresh chives, chopped,
    or other fresh herb like
    thyme or rosemary

TO MAKE THE ROAST

1.   Lightly season the roast with salt and pepper then liberally rub on the Smokin' Summer Spice Dry Rub (page 12).

2.   Let the roast sit at room temperature for 30-60 minutes, depending on the size.

3.   Sear the roast on all sides on a preheated gas grill.

4.   Leave only one of the burners on the right side of the grill on, but place the roast on the left side of the grill.

5.   Regulate the flame on the right side so that the temperature inside the barbecue with the cover closed is about 250-275°F.

6.   Cook the roast for about 30 minutes per pound or until the roast reaches your desired internal temperature on a meat thermometer (i.e., 125°F for rare; 135°F for medium rare; 145°F for medium; 155°F for medium well; 160°F for well done).

note > Cook time is approximate based on a small roast cooked to medium rare. Use a meat thermometer to ensure the roast is cooked to the level that you like. The cook time will vary greatly by the size of the roast.

7. Remember to loosely tent your roast with aluminum foil and let it stand at room temperature for 10-20 minutes (depending on the size of the roast) before carving and serving.

TO MAKE THE GARLIC CHILI BUTTER

1. Lightly sauté the garlic and ¼ cup butter together over medium-low heat. You only want to soften the garlic here and not brown it, so it will only take 1 or 2 minutes. Don't have your pan too hot.

2. Cool the garlic butter then mix it together with the 1 cup butter, chili paste, and the fresh herbs.

3. Place the prepared butter onto some plastic wrap and form into a log.

4. Refrigerate until the shape of the log stays intact, but take the butter out of the fridge to warm up to room temperature before serving in slices over the hot prime rib roast.

Honey Garlic Meatballs

PREP TIME **30 MINUTES** | COOK TIME **40 MINUTES** | SERVES **6**

FOR THE SAUCE

2 tbsp olive oil

4 cloves garlic, minced

1 cup water

1 cup honey

½ cup low sodium soy sauce

½ tsp Chinese five-spice powder

½ tsp black pepper, coarsely ground

2 tbsp cornstarch dissolved in ¼ cup water, as a thickening slurry

FOR THE MEATBALLS

1 cup bread crumbs, lightly packed

¼ cup milk

2 lbs coarsely ground lean pork or beef (or half & half of both)

1 egg

4 tbsp green onion, finely chopped

2 tbsp fresh ginger, grated (substitute 2 tsp powdered ginger if necessary)

2 cloves garlic, minced

1 tsp black pepper

1 tsp ground dried thyme

1 tsp kosher salt

½ tsp ground cumin

This is a go-to recipe at our house. Use either beef or pork to pair with the easiest, most delicious honey garlic sauce you'll find. I sometimes make extra sauce, especially if serving the meatballs with steamed rice or thin noodles.

It's a great dish to double or triple when you are feeding a crowd or to take along to a potluck dinner. I've even served them as party finger food with toothpicks, and believe me, they never last long!

TO MAKE THE SAUCE

1. Heat the olive oil in a small saucepan over medium heat.

2. Add the minced garlic and sauté for only 1 minute or so until it softens but does not brown.

3. Add the water, honey, soy sauce, five-spice powder, and pepper. (Do not add salt, there is plenty in the soy sauce.)

4. Let this mixture simmer for a few minutes then thicken with the slurry of cornstarch and water. Stir constantly as you add the slurry to the sauce. Cook for an additional minute before taking the sauce off the heat.

TO MAKE THE MEATBALLS

1. Pour the milk over the bread crumbs to soak while you gather the rest of the ingredients.

2. Put all ingredients in a large bowl and mix together well.

3. Form into 2-inch balls. Keeping your hands wet with cold water prevents the mixture from sticking to your hands.

4. Brown the meatballs on all sides in a non-stick frying pan for about 10 minutes. You want to get some good colour on them.

5. Place the meatballs in a small covered casserole dish and pour the sauce over them. Bake in a preheated 350°F oven for 30-40 minutes; the sauce should be bubbling well at this point.

6. Serve over steamed rice or thin Chinese noodles.

Rock Recipes has been known for great seafood recipes from the very beginning. Traditional recipes and new recipes alike take equal billing on our website.

Some, though, like the Cod au Gratin from the first *Rock Recipes* cookbook, take on a life of their own. I can't remember a book signing or other public event in years, where someone did not mention and compliment that recipe.

Here, we feature some contenders that deserve the same accolades. From an indulgent Creamy Seafood Chowder to Super Simple Shrimp Scampi or dinner party ready Prosciutto-Wrapped Cod, here you'll find a delicious dish for any occasion.

seafood

Super Simple Shrimp Scampi

PREP TIME **10 MINUTES** | COOK TIME **10 MINUTES** | SERVES **4**

What I love about this dish is that you can have it on the table in under 20 minutes and be serving this succulent shrimp scampi in practically the time it takes the family to come to the table. At the same time, it's elegant enough for a dinner party or a date night in. Serve over fresh pasta for a special touch.

---

6   tbsp butter

6   tbsp extra virgin olive oil

3   cloves garlic, minced

1½ lbs large uncooked shrimp, peeled and deveined

salt and pepper to season

juice of ½ lemon

2   oz white wine

¼   tsp red chili flakes (optional)

¼   cup fresh parsley, chopped, or any other mild herb you prefer, like tarragon, fennel leaves, cilantro, or oregano

zest of ½ lemon

350 g (one package) fresh linguine or fettuccine, cooked

lemon wedges, for garnish

freshly grated Parmesan, Romano, or Asiago cheese (optional)

1. Melt butter with the olive oil in a sauté pan over medium heat.

2. Add the chopped garlic for just about 30 seconds before adding a single layer of shrimp. Season with salt and pepper. Do not crowd your pan. If you are cooking a large number of shrimp, do them in smaller batches.

3. Cook the shrimp for only about 1 minute per side, depending on the size. Be careful not to overcook the shrimp.

4. Remove the shrimp from the pan and add the lemon juice, wine, and chili flakes, if desired.

5. Cook the sauce down to about half and return the shrimp to the pan along with the herbs and lemon zest. Toss together for another 1-2 minutes before tossing in the cooked pasta.

6. Serve with lemon wedges for garnish. Top with freshly grated cheese, if desired.

Prosciutto-Wrapped Cod
with Mediterranean Salsa

PREP TIME **30 MINUTES** | COOK TIME **20 MINUTES** | SERVES **4**

Prosciutto is probably my favourite cured meat of all time. Paired with beautiful, fresh North Atlantic cod, this recipe was a no-brainer for me.

This elegant dish served with a Mediterranean-inspired salsa is a perfect lighter choice for a dinner party.

There's nothing better than a recipe that's easy but impressive. This recipe is exactly that.

---

4   pieces cod fillet, thick cut, about 6 oz each

12 slices prosciutto, thin cut

black pepper to season the fish

FOR THE MEDITERRANEAN SALSA

2   large vine-ripened tomatoes, deseeded and diced small

¼   cup kalamata olives, pitted

2   tbsp capers, roughly chopped

1   tbsp chopped fresh herbs (oregano, dill, tarragon, thyme, or chives)

1   clove garlic, finely minced

juice of ½ lemon

zest of ½ lemon, finely grated

pinch chili flakes (optional)

pinch salt and pepper

TO MAKE THE MEDITERRANEAN SALSA

1.   Simply toss all of the ingredients together well in a glass bowl. Let stand for 20 minutes or so at room temperature while you prepare the fish. Toss the salsa a few times to ensure a good blending of the flavours.

TO MAKE THE FISH

1.   First lay 3 pieces of prosciutto on a cutting board. Slightly overlap the pieces, with two pieces in one direction and the third slice overlapping the two at the top of the shortest side.

2.   Lay a piece of cod on the third slice of prosciutto and roll gently but tightly in the 3 overlapping pieces.

3.   Repeat for the other 3 pieces of cod.

note > The wrapped fish can be cooked on an outdoor gas grill, in a cast iron grill pan, or in an oven-safe sauté pan. However you choose to cook it, the grill or the pan should be lightly oiled with canola oil and preheated to just above medium heat.

4.   Lay the pieces of fish on the grill or in the pan with the seam side of the prosciutto down. Grill or sauté for only 1-2 minutes on each side.

5. If using an outdoor grill, leave only one burner on and move the fish pieces to the opposite side, off of direct heat. Close the lid and cook for 10-15 minutes or until the fish is completely cooked through.

6. If using a stovetop method, after searing the outsides, place the pan in a preheated 350°F oven for 10-15 minutes until the fish is completely cooked through.

7. Allow the fish pieces to rest for 5 minutes before serving them with the salsa.

Scallops au Gratin

PREP TIME **20 MINUTES** | COOK TIME **30 MINUTES** | SERVES **4**

This dish was adapted from my incredibly popular Cod au Gratin recipe, featured in my first cookbook. I decided to make a version using my favourite seafood, scallops.

I kept it simple using only a creamy cheese sauce flavoured with garlic and fresh thyme, then topped with more cheese and some buttery breadcrumbs. The result was utterly delicious.

Scallops au Gratin makes an indulgent appetizer course, or a special lunchtime meal served with a side salad and crusty bread.

---

2 cups milk

¼ cup butter

2 cloves garlic, finely minced

4 tbsp flour

pinch salt and pepper to season

2 cups grated mild cheese, separated into 2 portions (I use a Swiss cheese like Gruyère, Jarlsberg, or Emmenthal)

20 large scallops

1 tsp fresh thyme, chopped

1 cup bread crumbs, toasted

2 tbsp butter, melted

1. Preheat the oven to 350°F.

2. Scald the milk in the microwave for about 4-5 minutes until just under the boiling point.

3. Meanwhile, in a medium saucepan melt the butter over low heat and add the garlic. Cook for only 1 minute so that the garlic softens but doesn't brown.

4. Add the flour and cook together for 2 minutes. The flour mixture should appear foamy. Again, do not let this brown.

5. Slowly pour in the scalded milk, whisking constantly.

6. Cook until the sauce begins to thicken. Season with salt and pepper to taste.

7. Stir in 1 cup of the grated cheese.

8. Arrange the scallops in the bottom of 4 small, individual gratin dishes. A small glass casserole dish about the size of a loaf pan will also work if making this in a single dish.

9. Sprinkle the chopped thyme over the scallops.

10. Spoon the sauce over the scallops. Top with the remaining grated cheese.

11. Mix the bread crumbs with the melted butter and sprinkle over the cheese.

12. Place the individual gratin dishes on a baking sheet.

13. Bake for about 30 minutes at 350°F until the sauce is bubbling and the top has evenly browned. Serve immediately.

Orange Hoisin Shrimp and Noodles

PREP TIME **5 MINUTES** | COOK TIME **10 MINUTES** | SERVES **4**

1 lb shrimp, shelled and cleaned

salt and pepper to season

3 tbsp olive oil

3 cloves garlic, minced

½ cup hoisin sauce

½ cup orange juice

4 tbsp rice vinegar

2 tbsp orange juice concentrate

2 tbsp soy sauce

1 tbsp fresh ginger root, grated

1 tbsp toasted sesame oil

½ tsp chili flakes, more or less to taste

½ tsp Chinese five-spice powder

¼ tsp black pepper

1 cup red pepper, chopped

½ lb Chinese noodles, cooked and drained

Keeping shrimp in the freezer is one of my secret weapons when it comes to quick, easy, and delicious dinner ideas.

This super quick, orange and hoisin shrimp recipe is on the table before you can even decide what to order off a takeout menu. It's a busy day lifesaver meal and a go-to recipe at our house whenever we need something fast.

1. Season the shrimp with salt, then lightly sauté in the olive oil for only 3-4 minutes over medium-high heat. Remove from the pan and set aside.

2. Add the garlic to the pan and sauté for only 1 minute to slightly soften the garlic, then add the remaining ingredients except the red pepper.

3. Simmer for just a few minutes until the sauce is thick enough to coat the back of a metal spoon, then add the shrimp back to the pan along with the red pepper.

4. After 1 minute, add the cooked noodles and toss well before serving.

Creamy Seafood Chowder

PREP TIME **30 MINUTES** | COOK TIME **50 MINUTES** | SERVES **8 OR MORE**

An utter feast of delicious fish and seafood in a beautifully seasoned, creamy broth. I've used a few tricks to make this recipe great, the first being not using too much flour in the roux so that the chowder isn't too thick. The real key to any successful creamy seafood chowder, however, is not to overcook the fish.

When done right, a good creamy seafood chowder makes for one of my favourite elegant lunches.

---

4   strips thick cut, smoked bacon, chopped small

2   tbsp butter

1   small white onion, finely diced

2   cloves garlic, minced

2   tbsp flour

3   cups low sodium seafood stock (some people prefer a light chicken stock)

3   cups whole milk

2   large bay leaves

½   tsp coarse black pepper

½   tsp dried summer savoury (thyme can be substituted)

½   tsp salt

zest of ½ large lemon, chopped

3 lbs assorted diced fish and seafood (I've used cod, shrimp, salmon, and mussels)

1½ cups whipping cream

1. Crisp cook the chopped bacon in the bottom of a large Dutch oven.

2. Remove the bacon and half the bacon fat. I like to hold back a little of the crisp bacon to garnish the top.

3. Over medium heat, add the butter to the remaining fat along with the onions and garlic, and sauté until the onions soften but do not brown.

4. Add the flour and continue to cook for 1-2 minutes. Do not let the flour brown. If it starts to brown, add the seafood stock immediately to stop the cooking action, stirring constantly.

5. While stirring constantly, add the seafood stock.

6. Next add the milk, bay leaves, pepper, savoury, salt, and lemon zest. Taste the broth to see if it needs additional salt.

7. Simmer the broth for 20 minutes before adding the seafood and simmering slowly for an additional 10 minutes. You really want a very gentle simmer. You are practically poaching the fish in this case. The result will be a much better presentation if the chunks of seafood remain whole.

8. Finally, add the whipping cream to finish the chowder and just bring it back to the boil before serving immediately. Garnish with reserved bacon pieces.

tip > My presentation method is to use a slotted spoon to remove the seafood chunks to the centres of shallow bowls, then add the broth around the rest of the bowl.

notes >

If you are using mussels in the recipe, you can keep them in the shell, especially if they are small, but if you want to add them without the shell, simply steam them for about 3 minutes until they open up. They can finish cooking in the broth when you add them with the other seafood. This is my preferred method because I don't want to leave unopened mussels in my chowder. You should always discard a mussel that does not open when cooked.

Some people prefer to add potatoes to seafood chowder. I sometimes do if serving the dish as a complete meal but mostly don't if I'm serving it as an appetizer. If using potatoes, choose yellow, waxy potatoes and not starchier potatoes like russets or blue potatoes, which will likely add additional thickening to the soup. I parboil the potatoes for 10 minutes then let them cool for a few minutes before dicing them into bite-sized pieces. I add the potatoes during the last 10 minutes of the simmering of the broth.

If using fresh herbs in the broth instead of dried, you can double the amount, except for bay leaves.

Parmesan Shrimp or Scallops

PREP TIME **15 MINUTES** | COOK TIME **5 MINUTES** | SERVES **4**

This is a versatile recipe you can use to cook either shrimp or scallops...or both! Pair with a nice steak to complete one of the tastiest surf-and-turf meals you'll try. That is a favourite of mine for Father's Day or any celebration meal.

On their own, these shrimp and scallops are delicious dipped in a homemade Caesar salad dressing. Pile them onto a sub roll for an Italian-inspired po' boy sandwich too!

---

canola oil for frying

1½ cups fine dry bread crumbs

½ cup Parmesan cheese, finely grated

½ tsp black pepper, coarsely ground

12 large scallops, at room temperature

12 large shrimp, at room temperature

salt and pepper to season

½ cup all-purpose flour

1 egg + ½ tbsp water

Caesar salad dressing for dip (optional)

1. Preheat the canola oil in a deep fryer, or in a cast iron Dutch oven or pan to 350°F.

2. Mix the bread crumbs, Parmesan cheese, and black pepper together well. I do this in my food processor to ensure that the cheese is a consistent size with the bread crumbs.

3. Season the shrimp and scallops with salt and pepper and then roll them in the plain flour to coat them.

4. Next, whisk together the egg and water to make an egg wash.

5. One at a time, dip the flour-coated shrimp and scallops into the egg wash and then into the Parmesan and bread crumb coating. Press them firmly into the crumb coating on all sides to get a good even coating.

6. Lay them on a parchment-lined baking sheet while you complete coating the rest of the seafood.

7. Drop them into the preheated fryer and cook for only about 5 minutes or until they are evenly golden brown.

8. Serve with Caesar salad dressing as a dip, if you like.

tip > It is best to have your shrimp and/or scallops near room temperature before cooking so that they do not cool down the oil too much. This is often the cause of deep-fried items absorbing too much oil and not being perfectly crispy.

Orange Five-Spiced Glazed Salmon

PREP TIME **15 MINUTES** | COOK TIME **20 MINUTES** | SERVES **4**

Here's one of those recipes that resulted when it seemed as though there was nothing in the fridge. Many of my most successful recipes start in that very same way.

A few simple ingredients thrown together to create a tasty salmon glaze saved us from a boring dinner and created a favourite recipe!

Inspired by teriyaki salmon, the addition of some bright citrus and Asian spice flavours made this a dish to remember.

---

4 six-ounce salmon fillet portions, about 1½ inches thick

salt and pepper to season

FOR THE GLAZE

1½ cups orange juice

¼ cup low sodium soy sauce

2 tbsp fresh ginger, grated

1 tsp Chinese five-spice powder

1 tsp sesame oil (or a few drops to taste)

½ tsp pepper

YOU WILL ALSO NEED

1 tsp cornstarch dissolved in a splash of water as a slurry

1. In a small pot, bring all of the glaze ingredients to a boil and simmer for 5 minutes before thickening with the cornstarch slurry.

2. Preheat the oven to 425°F.

3. Place the salmon fillets on a parchment-lined baking sheet, season with salt and pepper, and bake for about 10 minutes.

4. At this point, begin brushing the glaze on the salmon and returning it to the oven for about 2-3 minutes between coatings. I normally glaze it about 3 times.

5. You can always add more of the sauce to the fish when serving.

Penne Pasta Salad *with* Shrimp

Any type of pasta salad is a terrific make-ahead dish, especially for entertaining. Using low fat mayo also keeps it more calorie-wise than most pasta salad recipes.

Penne may just be my favourite pasta to use in pasta salad. The larger pasta pieces make it easier and less messy to eat too, plus the ridges hold on to the delicious dressing very well.

This simple and fresh shrimp pasta salad is terrific to serve with cold cuts, grilled chicken, fish, or as an ideal BBQ side dish.

---

3 cups dry penne pasta

1 cup cooked cocktail shrimp

1 small red pepper, finely diced

3 tbsp chives or cilantro, chopped

FOR THE GLAZE

¾ cup low fat mayonnaise

zest of 1 large lime, finely grated or chopped

1 clove garlic, very finely minced

3 tsp red Thai chilis, finely chopped (or 2 tsp crushed chili paste)

pinch of salt and pepper

1. Prepare the pasta as directed, adding a good pinch of salt to the water. Remove from heat and drain; let stand for 10 minutes or so, stirring occasionally.

2. Prepare the dressing simply by stirring all of the ingredients together well.

3. Pour the dressing over the pasta along with the shrimp, red pepper, and chives. Toss well. Chill before serving.

As in my other cookbooks, this chapter is all about avoiding the dinnertime dreads. Too often with many folks, dinner has become just one more thing to add to the list of things that occupy our busy lives.

It doesn't have to be that way, though. These recipes are deliciously designed to beat mealtime stress with just a little pre-planning. From Honey Ginger Pork Chops to budget-stretching Leftover Chicken Spaghetti, these dishes will have dinner on the table in no time.

So take a breath, exhale, and get dinner back to time enjoyed with family and friends around the table, just as it should be.

quick & easy dinners

Mongolian Beef

PREP TIME **20 MINUTES** | COOK TIME **10 MINUTES** | SERVES **6 REGULAR OR 4 LARGE SERVINGS**

Here is a Chinese takeout recipe that you can easily make at home. Mongolian Beef is one of the most popular dishes in many Chinese food restaurants in North America.

People love this dish for its balance of sweet and salty flavours, and this recipe has just a little extra zing. It's a quick and easy choice that lets you skip the takeout!

FOR THE SAUCE

¾ cup water

½ cup hoisin sauce

¼ cup brown sugar

¼ cup low sodium soy sauce

3 tbsp rice wine vinegar

2 tbsp fresh ginger, grated

2 tsp crushed chili paste or chili flakes to taste, optional

2 tbsp vegetable oil

3 cloves garlic, minced

FOR THE BEEF

1½ pounds beef steak (flank steak, rib-eye steak, or striploin steak are all good choices)

⅓ cup cornstarch, maybe a little more

about 1 cup vegetable oil, for frying

1 cup water chestnuts, sliced, about 1 can rinsed

1 cup bell peppers, chopped

TO MAKE THE SAUCE

1. In a small bowl or large measuring cup, stir together all the ingredients except the garlic and vegetable oil.

2. Heat the vegetable oil over medium heat and lightly sauté the garlic for only 1 minute, so that it softens but does not brown. (I like to make the sauce in a large sauté pan so that it reduces and thickens more quickly.)

3. Add the combined ingredients to the pan all at once and simmer for 5 minutes or so, until the sauce begins to thicken. Turn off the heat and set aside until the beef is cooked.

TO MAKE THE BEEF

1. Remove the beef from the fridge at least 30 minutes before preparing this recipe. Using beef straight from the fridge cools down the oil too much when frying.

2. Cut the beef across the grain into ¼-inch thick strips.

3. Dredge both sides of the beef strips with cornstarch and let them sit for 10 minutes, so that the cornstarch adheres to the meat. (You can start putting the sauce together while the beef sits.)

4. Heat the oil in a hot wok to 375°F. Fry the beef in about 3 batches, so that it cooks very quickly. It only takes about 1 minute or so to flash-fry the beef.

5. Pour off the oil from the wok completely.

6. Add the beef back to the wok with the vegetables and sauce, and simmer for only a few minutes before serving over steamed rice or your favourite noodles.

to make it as a stir-fry >

The cornstarch flash-frying does help to evenly coat the beef in the glistening sauce, but if you want to avoid the fried version of this recipe, try making it as a stir-fry instead.

1. Prepare the sauce first, so that it is properly reduced and thickened.

2. Add 3 tbsp vegetable oil to a hot wok and quickly stir-fry the beef before immediately adding the vegetables and sauce and simmering for a few additional minutes to heat the vegetables through.

3. The critical thing is not to overcook the beef. The wok should be as hot as possible and the beef need only be quickly stir-fried for a minute or so until it loses the pink colour to be fully cooked. The extra few minutes of simmering will guarantee that it is anyway.

Amatriciana Pasta *with* Chicken

PREP TIME **30 MINUTES** | COOK TIME **40 MINUTES** | SERVES **6 OR MORE**

This dish is a version of chicken fettuccine with blush tomato sauce. It's a simple but delicious pasta dish that you can make any day of the week but that's impressive enough to serve at a dinner party too.

The smokiness of the bacon, the sweetness of the tomatoes and peppers, the slight saltiness of the capers and olives, plus the added richness of the cream to the sauce all combine to make one impressive dish. It may not be strictly authentic Italian, but it is truly delicious.

6	boneless, skinless chicken breasts
3	tbsp olive oil
4-6	cloves garlic, finely chopped
2	cans (19 oz) of Roma tomatoes (I purée tomatoes in the food processor)
1	red pepper, diced
1	large tomato, diced
1½	cups mushrooms, sliced
½	cup kalamata olives, pitted and chopped
8	strips smoked bacon, crisp cooked and crumbled
4	tbsp fresh basil or oregano, chopped (use half the amount if using dried herbs)
2	tbsp brown sugar
2	tbsp capers, roughly chopped
1	tsp chili flakes, or to taste
1	tsp salt, or to taste, for seasoning
½	tsp black pepper, coarsely ground, or to taste, for seasoning
½	cup whipping cream
½	cup grated Parmesan, Romano, or Asiago cheese
1-1½	lbs fresh fettuccine

1. Flatten the chicken breasts to about ½-inch thickness. Season both sides with salt and pepper.

2. Grill chicken breasts on the barbeque, or pan-fry them in olive oil. Slice or dice them and set aside. (Chicken breasts can be cooked in advance. I have even cooked them the day before and used them cold out of the fridge.)

3. Heat about 3 tbsp olive oil in a large Dutch oven over medium-low heat.

4. Add the garlic and cook for 1 minute. Add puréed canned tomatoes, peppers, fresh tomato, mushrooms, olives, bacon, fresh basil or oregano, brown sugar, capers, chili flakes, and salt and pepper to taste. I like lots of pepper in this recipe.

5. Simmer the sauce, uncovered, for 20 minutes, add whipping cream, and simmer for 5 minutes more.

6. Add the chicken to the sauce and simmer for 5 more minutes, uncovered.

7. Stir in the cheese and remove from heat.

8. Serve over cooked linguine, or fettuccine, and top with grated Parmesan or Romano cheese.

Vegetarian Quinoa Chili

PREP TIME **15 MINUTES** | COOK TIME **1 HOUR** | SERVES **6-8**

2 tbsp olive oil

1 cup carrot, diced small

1 cup celery, diced small

1 cup red onion, diced small

3 cloves garlic, minced

4 cups canned tomatoes, diced

1 cup fresh or frozen corn kernels

3 tbsp chili powder

1 tbsp brown sugar

2 tsp chipotle powder

2 tsp ground cumin

1 tsp dried thyme

½ tsp black pepper

½ tsp salt to season

1 cup cooked quinoa (about ¼ cup dry quinoa slowly simmered in ½ cup salted water)

2 cups cooked kidney beans (rinsed if you are using canned)

This chili is the ideal choice for a "Meatless Monday" dinner. Like many families, we like to have a vegetarian dish now and then as a healthy option. It's also a chance to experiment and keep our dinner menus varied and tasty.

It's also a dish that's one of our favourites to serve when entertaining vegetarian guests. This chili is so chock full of flavour and nutrition, complete with the extra protein from quinoa, you may never miss the meat at all!

1.   In a Dutch oven or large saucepan over medium heat, add the olive oil, carrot, celery, red onion, and garlic.

2.   Sauté until the onions soften, then add the tomatoes, corn, chili powder, brown sugar, chipotle powder, cumin, thyme, black pepper, and salt.

3.   Simmer slowly for 20 minutes then add the cooked quinoa and kidney beans.

4.   Simmer for only another 10 minutes or so before serving with a dollop of low fat sour cream or Greek yogurt.

Asian Glazed Chicken

PREP TIME **10** MINUTES | COOK TIME **1** HOUR **+ 2** HOURS MARINATING TIME | SERVES **6**

This recipe was inspired by the success of my Asian Glazed Pork Belly. A delicious, intensely tasty version of sticky chicken with a burst of several flavours from the Far East.

The marinade does double duty to first flavour the chicken before being boiled to become a tasty, sticky glaze. It is a real finger-licking good recipe that the whole family will enjoy.

---

3 lbs chicken pieces or boneless breasts

FOR THE MARINADE/GLAZE
¼ cup hoisin sauce (oyster sauce will work too)

¼ cup honey

¼ cup low sodium soy sauce

2 tbsp rice vinegar

1 tbsp fish sauce

1 tbsp fresh ginger, grated

2 tsp crushed chili paste (or 2 tsp finely minced fresh red chili)

1½ tsp Chinese five-spice powder

1 tsp black pepper

1. Mix all of the ingredients in the marinade together and pour over the chicken pieces in a large zip-lock bag.

2. Marinate in the fridge for several hours or overnight.

3. Preheat the oven to 350°F.

4. Remove the chicken pieces from the marinade and place them on a parchment paper-lined baking sheet. (Don't throw out the marinade!)

5. Roast the chicken pieces for about 20 minutes before brushing them with the glaze you make from the leftover marinade.

6. Pour the reserved marinade into your smallest saucepan. (You can add all the same ingredients again to make extra sauce/glaze for rice or noodles, if you like.)

7. Slowly simmer the marinade until it begins to become like a thin syrup, about maple syrup consistency.

8. In the last 40 minutes of roasting, begin to brush on layers of the glaze. I do this 4-6 times about every 10 minutes, to build good, flavourful, sticky glaze on the chicken pieces.

tip > This recipe can also be made on the grill. Since the chicken will cook faster on the grill, start glazing it after the first 5 minutes and continue to turn and glaze several times until the chicken is fully cooked.

Honey Ginger Pork Chops

PREP TIME **15 MINUTES** | COOK TIME **15 MINUTES** | SERVES **6**

A super simple glaze gets brushed repeatedly onto these perfectly cooked, juicy chops in one of the easiest and most flavourful pork chop recipes you'll ever try.

The great thing about the added glaze is that your pork chops can be cooked on the backyard grill, under the broiler, or pan seared. Coupled with a simple rice or pasta dish, this makes a great workday meal in only about 20 minutes!

---

6   pork loin chops
     (thick cut will work best)

FOR THE GLAZE

2   tbsp Dijon mustard

2   tbsp fresh ginger, grated

½   cup honey

½   tsp black pepper, freshly
     ground

½   tsp kosher salt

1.   Season the pork chops with salt and pepper and grill lightly for only a couple of minutes per side. (If pan searing the pork chops, cook them almost completely before draining off the excess oil and adding the glaze to the pan and turning the chops for a couple of minutes in the pan.)

2.   After turning once, begin brushing on the glaze, turning the pork chops every minute for about 5-6 minutes, or until they are completely cooked to about 160°F on a meat thermometer inserted into the centre.

3.   Let the pork chops rest for 5-10 minutes before serving.

TO MAKE THE GLAZE

1.   Simply simmer all the glaze ingredients together over medium-low heat for about 10 minutes. Watch the glaze carefully. You want a gentle simmer or the honey on the glaze will foam up considerably and possibly boil over.

Leftover Chicken Spaghetti

PREP TIME **10 MINUTES** | COOK TIME **20 MINUTES** | SERVES **4**

2 tbsp olive oil

3 cloves garlic, minced

4 cups puréed canned tomatoes (San Marzano if possible)

½ lb crisp cooked smoked bacon, chopped in small pieces

2 tbsp balsamic vinegar

1 tbsp brown sugar

1 tsp dried oregano

½ tsp smoked paprika

½ tsp pepper

½ tsp salt

¼ tsp chili flakes, optional

3 cups cooked chicken, diced

1 large bell pepper, diced small

4 servings cooked spaghetti pasta

¼ cup grated Parmesan cheese

This is a perfect recipe to transform leftover chicken or turkey into a flavourful and satisfying meal. Paired with a smokey bacon tomato sauce and whatever fresh veggies you have on hand, it's a great way to get a delicious dinner on the table quickly.

With recipes like this in mind, I always cook extra chicken and plan for leftovers as part of the week's menu.

Never cook twice when you can cook once. Embrace leftovers as a time-saving way to deliciously simplify meals.

1. Begin by making the sauce. In a medium saucepan heat 2 tbsp olive oil over medium-low and sauté the minced garlic for about 30 seconds.

2. Add the pureed tomatoes, bacon, balsamic vinegar, brown sugar, oregano, smoked paprika, pepper, salt, and chili flakes.

3. Simmer on low for about 20 minutes, adding the cooked diced chicken and bell peppers in the last 5 minutes of cooking time. Stir in the Parmesan cheese at the end.

4. Serve over the cooked spaghetti with a generous sprinkle of additional Parmesan cheese.

Orange Beef *with* Cashews

PREP TIME **10 MINUTES** | COOK TIME **15 MINUTES** | SERVES **4**

This is one of our family's favourite quick stir-fry recipes. It's incredibly versatile.

Use whatever veggies you have on hand, and adjust the chili to make it as spicy or as mild as you like. Both ways are delicious.

This dish is similar to a Chinese takeout dish, but ready at home in under 30 minutes. That's likely faster than ordering takeout with delivery!

- 3 tbsp peanut oil
- 2 cloves garlic, minced
- 1 lb beef tenderloin, or striploin steak, thinly sliced
- salt and pepper to season
- 1 cup red pepper, diced
- 1 cup orange juice
- zest of ½ an orange, finely minced
- 4 tbsp hoisin sauce
- 4 tbsp rice wine, or Chinese cooking wine
- 3 tbsp brown sugar
- 3 tbsp rice wine vinegar (or apple cider vinegar in a pinch)
- 2 tsp fresh ginger, grated (or ½ tsp powdered ginger)
- 2 tsp soy sauce
- 2 tsp toasted sesame oil
- 1 tsp chili paste (or ½ tsp chili flakes), optional or to taste
- 1 rounded tsp cornstarch, dissolved in 1 oz orange juice or water to make a slurry
- 2 oranges, peeled and sectioned (supreme; see note)
- ¾ cup cashews, toasted

1. Heat peanut oil in a wok over high heat.

2. Quickly add the garlic and beef, season with salt and pepper, and stir-fry for only about 1 minute.

3. Add the peppers and stir-fry for only about another 30 seconds. Remove the beef and peppers from the pan and set aside.

4. Add the orange juice and zest to the wok and simmer to reduce the orange juice volume by half.

5. In a small bowl, mix together the hoisin sauce, rice wine, brown sugar, rice wine vinegar, ginger, soy sauce, sesame oil, and chili paste.

note > Toasted sesame oil is usually sold in smaller bottles and has a darker colour than normal vegetable oil and a much more intense flavour. It's one of those ingredients where a little goes a long way, so don't overdo it.

6. Stir well and add to the reduced orange juice in the wok.

7. Simmer for a couple of minutes before returning the beef and peppers to the wok with the sauce.

8. Bring to a boil and thicken with the cornstarch slurry.

tip > You can add whatever vegetables you like to this recipe. We generally use what's on hand. Green onions, green beans, snow peas, broccoli, and especially water chestnuts all have made appearances in this dish from time to time.

9. Toss in the orange segments at the end to let them warm through before serving.

note > I like to supreme the oranges before adding them. This means removing the peel with a knife, then cutting out the orange segments, individually, leaving the surrounding tougher membranes behind. For larger oranges, I then cut each segment in half before adding at the end.

10. Serve over rice or noodles and sprinkle generously with the toasted cashews.

Sweet Chili Lime Chicken

PREP TIME **10** MINUTES | COOK TIME **45** MINUTES | SERVES **4-6**

This easy baked chicken is sweet, sticky, and citrusy with a little kick from the chili. It's the opposite of a boring chicken dinner.

Made with only a handful of ingredients, it's an easy and economical dish to keep in mind when you need a fresh meal idea.

---

1 whole chicken in pieces, or 3 lbs chicken pieces

FOR THE SAUCE

3 tbsp butter

3 cloves garlic, minced

½ cup honey

juice of 4 limes (½ cup juice)

2 tsp chili paste or to taste (or 1 tsp chili flakes)

½ tsp ground black pepper

½ tsp salt

1. Preheat the oven to 425°F. Line a baking pan, about 9x13 inches in size, with a couple of layers of heavy-duty aluminum foil and place the lined, empty pan in an oven to heat up for 5-10 minutes. This speeds up the cooking time and will help the sauce reduce in volume a little. Use a baking pan that will be large enough to fit all the chicken pieces without overcrowding but won't leave large open spaces. Using too large a baking dish can cause the sauce to be too shallow in the pan and burn easily.

2. In a small saucepan, melt the butter over medium-low heat.

3. Add the garlic and sauté for only 1 minute so that it softens but doesn't brown.

4. Add all remaining ingredients for the sauce and simmer slowly for 10 minutes.

5. Remove from heat to cool a little.

6. Cut the chicken into 8 pieces, trimming them well of excess skin and fat.

7. Lightly season the chicken pieces with additional salt and pepper. Remove the hot pan from the oven and place the chicken pieces in the pan.

8. Pour the prepared sauce evenly over the chicken, but don't submerge it more than halfway, as shown in the sidebar photo. Any remaining sauce can be used to pour over the completed chicken or over rice.

9. Return the pan to the 425°F oven and bake for 15 minutes. Remove from the oven and baste the chicken pieces with the sauce in the bottom of the pan.

10. Return to the oven for an additional 25-30 minutes or until a meat thermometer inserted into the centre of the thickest part of the breast and thighs reads 170°F.

11. Allow the chicken to rest for 5-10 minutes before serving.

Vegetarian Mushroom Burger
with Honey Dijon Mayo

PREP TIME **30** MINUTES **+ A FEW HOURS CHILLING TIME FOR THE BURGER MIXTURE**

COOK TIME **15** MINUTES | SERVES **6**

FOR THE MUSHROOM BURGERS

5	cups mushrooms, roughly chopped
3	tbsp butter or olive oil
2	large red onions
3	cloves garlic, minced
1½	cups cooked brown rice
1	cup ground oatmeal (grind large flake oats in the food processor, or you can use quick oats instead)
1	cup roughly mashed chickpeas
½	cup brown rice flour, plus a little more for dusting the patties before frying
4	tbsp soy sauce
1	tbsp fresh thyme (or 1-2 tsp dried thyme)
1	tsp crushed chili paste or hot sauce, or a pinch of chili flakes (more or less to taste)
1	tsp nutmeg, freshly ground
½	tsp black pepper, freshly ground
½	tsp kosher salt

FOR THE HONEY DIJON MAYO

¾	cup plain mayonnaise
2	tbsp whole grain Dijon mustard
1-2	tbsp honey to taste

This vegetarian mushroom burger recipe certainly is not short on flavour. Make them as burgers or sliders at parties or barbecues, and even the meat eaters will love them!

I developed this recipe by cherry-picking what I thought were the best attributes from a couple of vegetarian burger recipes I'd seen. The texture of the burger and the deep earthy flavour of the mushrooms really make this recipe special.

Even the meat eaters I've served them to thought they were absolutely delicious.

TO MAKE THE MUSHROOM BURGERS

1.   Sauté the mushrooms in the butter until the mushrooms are well browned and have shrunken down considerably. Remove from the pan and set aside.

2.   Sauté the onions and garlic together until fully softened.

3.   Add the onions and garlic to the food processor along with all of the other ingredients listed for the burger patties EXCEPT the mushrooms.

4.   Pulse together until well blended but not perfectly smooth. You want to leave some texture in the mix.

5.   You can quickly pulse in the mushrooms at this point, but I prefer to mix them in by hand. This helps maintain their meaty texture.

6.   Chill the mixture for a couple of hours or even overnight before using.

7. Form the mixture into 6 equal balls and roll the balls in brown rice flour, then form into burger patties.

8. Cook in a lightly oiled cast iron pan over medium heat until well browned on each side. Serve on toasted buns with lettuce and tomato and Honey Dijon Mayo.

TO MAKE THE HONEY DIJON MAYO

1. Simply mix together the ingredients, then serve on the finished burgers.

Sunday dinner is still an important weekly occurrence in our house, as it was in our family homes growing up. In my cookbooks and on my blog, I still promote a weekend family meal as the most important of the week.

As busy weekdays come and go, making time for dinner is still important as well, but admittedly often hard to accomplish every day. That's why Sunday dinner becomes even more important, because it's not just about the food, it's about catching up and reconnecting.

When you can do all of that while enjoying a delicious comfort food meal, well, that's even better.

slow-cooked sundays

Smoked Paprika Roast Lamb
with Summer Savoury Stuffing

PREP TIME **30** MINUTES | COOK TIME **2** HOURS | SERVES **8** OR MORE

This incredibly delicious recipe for tender roast leg of lamb has a flavourful smoked paprika and garlic rub on the outside, and a fragrant summer savoury and onion stuffing inside. It is an amazing Easter dinner idea, or for any special Sunday dinner.

4 lb boneless leg of lamb

FOR THE SUMMER SAVOURY STUFFING

1 small red onion, finely diced

3 cloves garlic, finely minced

¼ cup butter

4 cups coarse bread crumbs

2 tbsp dried summer savoury

½ tsp black pepper

pinch salt

1 egg, beaten

¼ cup vegetable stock or water

FOR THE SMOKED PAPRIKA RUB

2 tbsp smoked paprika

1 tbsp olive oil

1 tbsp Worcestershire sauce

3 cloves garlic, finely minced

½ tsp black pepper

½ tsp kosher salt

TO MAKE THE STUFFING

1. Sauté the onions and garlic in the butter over medium heat for just a few minutes until the onions have softened but not browned.

2. Toss together the bread crumbs with the summer savory, pepper, and salt. Next add the sautéed onions and garlic along with the butter from the pan.

3. Beat together the egg and vegetable stock, and pour over the bread crumb mixture. Mix the stuffing together with a wooden spoon until well combined.

TO MAKE THE LAMB

1. Lay the boneless leg of lamb on a cutting board, opening it up so that it is as flat as possible. Cut horizontally into the thickest parts of the roast but not all the way through, so that you can fold the cut sections back and even out the thickness of the meat. Alternatively, you can use a meat mallet to pound the roast to about 1-1½-inch thickness.

2. Press the stuffing together in handfuls and place it evenly along the centre line of the flattened roast.

3. Bring the sides of the roast up over the stuffing and tie with several lengths of butcher string to close. Use a couple of lengths of butcher string to tie the two ends closed as well, so that they cross the other strings at a 90-degree angle. This helps keep the stuffing inside and ensures more even cooking.

4. Mix together all of the ingredients for the rub, and spread the paste all over the roast. Use your fingers to rub it in evenly over all surfaces of the tied and stuffed lamb leg.

5. Let the rub marinate into the meat for 1 hour or so before roasting.

6. Preheat the oven to 400°F.

7. Place the prepared roast in a shallow roasting pan or on a parchment-lined baking sheet to roast for 20 minutes.

8. Reduce the heat to 325°F and continue to roast for about 90 minutes or until a meat thermometer inserted into the centre of the stuffing reaches 160°F, which would indicate the lamb is cooked to medium-well.

9. Remove the roast from the oven and loosely tent it with aluminum foil. Allow the roast to rest for 20 minutes before carving.

Black Bean, Sausage, and Duck Cassoulet

PREP TIME **30 MINUTES** | COOK TIME **90 MINUTES** | SERVES **4-6**

This simple, slow-cooked French comfort food stew is one of the best cold weather meals there is, with a deeply flavoured, rich broth and wholesome, nutritious black beans too.

A cassoulet (pronounced cass-oo-lay) may sound fancy, but it is really more of a simple stew. If you are not partial to duck, or it's difficult to find in your location, you can easily substitute chicken legs.

2-3 duck legs

pinch salt and pepper to season

1 lb good quality pork sausage (garlic and herb or mild Italian are good choices)

1 large red onion, finely diced

2 stalks celery, finely diced

4 cloves garlic, minced

2 cups cooked black beans (if using canned, rinse and drain well)

1½ cups chicken or duck stock

1½ cups canned tomatoes, puréed

4 large carrots, cut in 3-inch sticks

2 tbsp fresh thyme, chopped

3 bay leaves

1. Preheat the oven to 325°F.

2. Season the duck legs on both sides with salt and pepper. In a cast iron frying pan, brown the duck legs and sausages over medium-high heat then set aside.

3. Reduce the heat to medium and add the onions, celery, and garlic to the pan. Lightly season with salt and pepper and cook until the onions have softened but not browned.

4. Transfer the cooked onions, celery, and garlic to a large, covered Dutch oven or roasting pan. Add the black beans, chicken stock, canned tomatoes, carrots, thyme, and bay leaves. Stir together and add the sausages and duck legs on top of the beans and vegetables.

5. Cover and place in the preheated oven and cook for 2-2½ hours or until the duck is tender enough to fall off the bone.

6. Serve the duck pieces and sausages on top of the black beans. Another suggestion is to shred the duck, slice the sausages, and mix both through the beans and vegetables. This can be then spooned on top of some plain steamed rice to serve.

Honey Garlic Sticky Ribs

PREP TIME **20 MINUTES** | COOK TIME **8 HOURS** | SERVES **6**

Slowly cooked to tender perfection and glazed with layers of sweet, sticky garlic glaze, these are the kind of ribs you just can't stop eating!

Perfect for dinner with some rice or noodles or as game-day grub to share with friends. This is a recipe that's firmly planted in the finger-licking good category.

3-4 lbs pork back or side ribs

FOR THE DRY RUB

2 tbsp powdered ginger

1 tbsp onion powder

1½ tsp kosher salt

1 tsp garlic powder

1 tsp ground thyme

½ tsp black pepper

½ tsp ground nutmeg

¼-½ tsp cayenne pepper

FOR THE GLAZE

2 tbsp olive oil

4 cloves garlic, minced

1 cup honey

¼ cup soy sauce (low sodium is best)

1 tsp ground black pepper

TO MAKE THE DRY RUB

1. Mix together all ingredients well.

TO MAKE THE GLAZE

1. In a medium saucepan, add the 2 tbsp olive oil and minced garlic. Cook over medium heat to soften the garlic, but do not let it brown.

2. Add the honey, soy sauce, and black pepper.

3. Simmer very slowly for about 20 minutes until the sauce reduces and thickens slightly. Watch this carefully as it simmers because it can foam up over the pot very easily. Remove from heat and allow to cool for a few minutes.

TO MAKE THE RIBS

1. There is a thin membrane called silver skin on the back of all pork ribs that I like to remove first. If left on, it will shrink during cooking and cause the ribs to curl. It also prevents the spice mix from seasoning the underside of the ribs. I push a butter knife between the silver skin and the first bone on the rack of ribs to loosen the skin, then I poke my finger into the slit the knife has made, grasp the silver skin, and pull it off all the way down the length of the rack of ribs.

2. Liberally rub the spice mix all over the surface of the pork ribs on both sides. Cover with plastic wrap and place in the fridge for several hours or, as I prefer, overnight. You can of

course cook them immediately, but you get better flavour penetration into the meat if you do the rub in advance. The ribs will be delicious either way, if you are pressed for time.

3.   Place the ribs, uncovered, on a wire rack over a baking sheet and place in a 225°F oven for 8-9 hours, depending on the thickness of the ribs. Baby back ribs tend to take less time than side ribs, for example.

4.   In the last couple of hours of cooking time, begin brushing on the glaze and turning the ribs every 30 minutes or so. You can continuously brush on layers of glaze for as long and as often as you like to build up the sticky glaze to your taste.

5.   When a bone from the ribs is easily and cleanly able to be pulled away from the meat, then they are done.

6.   Let the ribs rest for 10 minutes before serving.

Worcestershire Butter Roast Beef

PREP TIME **10 MINUTES** | COOK TIME **80 MINUTES** | SERVES **10 OR MORE**

My idea for this roast beef came from wanting to marinate a roast in Worcestershire sauce, without the meat being overwhelmed by the flavour of the marinade. My solution was a compound butter to act as a marinade. The Worcestershire sauce as well as garlic, thyme, pepper, and salt, all get suspended in the butter. This allows their flavour to slowly infuse into the meat overnight. The next day all you have to do is pull the beef from the fridge, let it sit to room temperature, then roast to tender, buttery perfection.

4	lb beef roast (prime rib, tenderloin, or striploin roast is best)
⅓	cup soft butter
1½	tbsp Worcestershire sauce
1	tbsp English-style mustard (optional)
3	cloves garlic, minced
1	tsp dried thyme
½	tsp black pepper, coarsely ground
½	tsp kosher salt

1. Cream together the butter, Worcestershire sauce, mustard, garlic, thyme, pepper, and salt.

2. Using cold wet hands, pat the butter all over the roast (see sidebar photo.)

3. Cover in plastic wrap and let stand in the fridge for up to 24 hours.

4. Take the roast out of the fridge 60-90 minutes before roasting. This ensures a more even cooking of the beef.

5. Preheat the oven to 425°F.

6. Place the beef on a roasting rack in an aluminum foil-lined, shallow roasting pan, and roast, uncovered, for 20 minutes.

7. Reduce heat to 375°F and roast, uncovered, for up to 1 hour or until the roast reaches the internal temperature required for the doneness you prefer. (See notes for temperature guide.) Baste the roast a couple of times with the butter and pan drippings during the cooking time.

8. Remove the roast from the oven and loosely tent it with aluminum foil. Leave it for 20-30 minutes before carving. This is an essential step to let the meat relax and retain its juices. Carving any roast too early can make all of the internal juices run off rapidly.

9. After the roast has rested, slice thinly and serve.

internal temperature guide for beef roast >

Medium-rare 145°F (63°C)

Medium 160°F (71°C)

Well done 170°F (77°C)

Stuffed Chicken Thighs *with* Mozzarella, Prosciutto & Spicy Tomato Compote

PREP TIME **30 MINUTES** | COOK TIME **45 MINUTES** | SERVES **4**

Chicken thighs are another ingredient that I think is much underused. Well-trimmed of excess fat, they are an economical and flavourful way to get dinner on the table.

These stuffed chicken thighs are the kind of recipe I love because of the simple ingredients, ease of preparation, and versatility. This is easy enough for a delicious family dinner, but fancy enough to serve at your next dinner party too.

---

2 lbs boneless, skinless chicken thighs (about 8 thighs)

FOR THE SPICY TOMATO COMPOTE

6 tbsp olive oil

4 cloves garlic, minced

8 large ripe tomatoes, diced

2 tbsp brown sugar

1 tsp crushed chili sauce or ½ tsp chili flakes (or to taste)

salt and pepper to season

6 tbsp balsamic vinegar

FOR THE STUFFED CHICKEN THIGHS

salt and pepper to season

6 oz prosciutto, very thinly sliced

8 oz fresh mozzarella

2 oz Parmesan cheese (optional, to add when serving)

TO MAKE THE SPICY TOMATO COMPOTE

1. In a large sauté pan, sauté the garlic in the oil over medium heat for just 1 minute, until the garlic is softened but not browned.

2. Add the tomatoes, brown sugar, chili sauce, salt, and pepper.

3. Continue to cook until the tomatoes soften and the compote reduces to a jam-like consistency.

4. Add the balsamic vinegar in the final 1-2 minutes before serving.

5. Keep warm until ready to serve over the chicken thighs.

TO MAKE THE STUFFED CHICKEN THIGHS

1. Preheat the oven to 375°F.

2. Debone and skin the chicken thighs and trim of all visible fat.

3. Lay the trimmed chicken thighs on a cutting board and lightly season the inside only with salt and pepper. The prosciutto will season the outside of the chicken thighs, so be careful to add only a little salt.

4. Place a 1-oz block of fresh mozzarella cheese at the centre of each chicken thigh. Fold the chicken meat around the cheese to cover it.

5. Wrap each chicken thigh completely in the thinly sliced prosciutto, then place on a parchment paper-lined baking sheet, keeping them separated by about 2 inches. You can keep the prosciutto tightly wrapped to the chicken by using a couple of toothpicks, if you like, but use the same number of toothpicks in each so that it's easy to remember to remove them all before serving.

6. Bake at 375°F for about 45-55 minutes depending on the size of the thighs you are using. Use a meat thermometer to make sure the centres of the cooked pieces have hit 170°F. Over baking these can cause the cheese to ooze out onto the pan.

7. Serve over freshly cooked pasta, rice, or roasted potatoes with a sprinkle of grated Parmesan cheese.

St. John's Stout Braised Beef Ribs

PREP TIME **20 MINUTES** | COOK TIME **4 HOURS** | SERVES **6**

4 lbs beef ribs

salt and pepper to season

½ cup flour (approximate—only use enough to coat the ribs)

2-3 tbsp canola oil

12 oz stout beer (or other quality beer, or red wine)

4 cups beef stock (if not using homemade, choose a good quality, low sodium stock)

4 slices bacon, crisp-cooked and crumbled

1 red onion, minced

½ cup orange juice

½ whole nutmeg, grated

4 tbsp fresh rosemary, chopped

2 tbsp fresh thyme

3 cloves garlic, chopped

1 tsp cracked black pepper

¼ tsp ground cloves

1 cup fresh mushrooms, sliced (optional)

I don't know if there is a better comfort food than slow-braised beef ribs with good mashed potatoes. Of course, a rich, delicious gravy brings a lot to this comfort food classic too.

Inspired by a favourite stew made with a great local stout beer, I've used the same method and flavourful ingredients to create these perfect, tender, rich-tasting, slow-cooked ribs. They also create their own gravy as they slowly braise to unparalleled deliciousness.

1. Cut beef into individual ribs. Season the ribs with salt and pepper, then dredge them in plain flour before browning them in the canola oil in a large frying pan. Work in small batches so as not to crowd the pan. This will make browning the ribs easier.

2. Preheat the oven to 300°F. Transfer the browned beef ribs to a large covered roasting pan (I use a large enamel-covered turkey roaster).

3. Add the remaining ingredients, EXCEPT the mushrooms.

4. Place the covered roaster in the oven and roast for about 4 hours or until the meat easily pulls away from the bone. In the last 30 minutes of cooking time, you can add the mushrooms.

5. Once fully cooked, remove the ribs from the roasting pan and skim the fat from the jus/gravy. I find that a gravy strainer (fat separator) works very well for this. Serve with mashed potatoes and steamed vegetables, and the delicious jus/gravy.

Herb Crusted Pork Loin

PREP TIME **20 MINUTES** | COOK TIME **90 MINUTES** | SERVES **8 OR MORE**

This perfectly roasted pork loin is a great recipe for when you have a roast to serve a crowd. It's a simple but very flavourful preparation for an easy and succulent result.

The cook time will depend on the size of your roast. In general, 20 minutes per pound is a good guideline; however, always use a meat thermometer to check that pork is properly cooked to 160°F. It's a surefire way to never cook dry pork again.

---

3 lb (or larger) boneless pork loin roast

FOR THE HERB AND MUSTARD CRUST

4 tbsp coarse grain Dijon mustard

3 cloves garlic, minced

2 tbsp oregano

2 tbsp thyme

1 tbsp fresh rosemary, chopped

1 tbsp black pepper, coarsely ground

1 tsp kosher salt

1 tbsp Worcestershire sauce

1. Preheat oven to 350°F.

2. Mix together all of the ingredients for the herb crust into a paste.

3. Rub the paste over the entire surface of the pork loin roast.

4. Roast uncovered on a rack in a large roasting pan for about 20 minutes per pound or until the internal temperature of the roast reaches 160°F on a meat thermometer.

5. Allow roast to rest for 15 minutes after it comes out of the oven before carving and serving.

Maple Applesauce *on* Herb-Roasted Pork Loin

PREP TIME **30 MINUTES** | COOK TIME **80 MINUTES** | SERVES **8**

3 lb centre loin pork roast

FOR THE BRINE

8 cups water

½ cup brown sugar

¼ cup kosher salt

2 tbsp black peppercorns

3 bay leaves

3 cloves garlic, chopped

TO SEASON THE OUTSIDE OF THE PORK BEFORE ROASTING

1 tsp ground sage

½ tsp ground black pepper

½ tsp ground thyme

2 tbsp olive oil

FOR THE MAPLE APPLESAUCE

6 large apples (McIntosh is a good choice for applesauce)

¼ cup apple cider vinegar

¼ cup maple syrup (you can substitute brown sugar, if you prefer)

½ tsp cinnamon

¼ tsp nutmeg

pinch of salt

pinch of ground cloves (optional)

There's a couple of tricks to keeping a leaner cut of pork roast juicy. The first is to always use a meat thermometer to ensure it is succulent and cooked, but not overcooked. The second trick is to brine the pork, infusing flavour all the way through and ensuring it is extra juicy.

Apples and pork are a naturally delicious combination. A sweet and tangy maple-infused applesauce really complements this comfort food meal perfectly. A tasty choice for Sunday dinner.

---

1.   In a large glass or plastic bowl, dissolve the brown sugar and kosher salt into the water before adding the peppercorns, bay leaves, and chopped garlic.

2.   Submerge the pork loin roast into the brine. I usually place a small plate on top of the meat to weigh it down and keep it completely surrounded by the brining liquid. Cover the bowl with plastic wrap and place in the fridge for 24-48 hours.

3.   Remove the pork from the brining liquid and pat completely dry with paper towels.

4.   Mix together the sage, pepper, and thyme and sprinkle evenly over the entire surface of the roast.

5.   Finally, rub the olive oil all over the roast and place it on a rack in a roasting pan.

6.   Leave the roast at room temperature for 30-40 minutes before roasting. This helps to ensure a more evenly cooked roast.

7.   Roast in a preheated 375°F oven until the centre temperature reaches 160°F on a meat thermometer. My 3-lb roast took about 80 minutes.

8.   While still on the roasting rack, tent the roast loosely with aluminum foil and let rest for 15 minutes before carving. Serve with warm maple applesauce.

TO MAKE THE MAPLE APPLESAUCE

1.   Simmer all of the ingredients together for 25-30 minutes or until the apples break down and the liquid has mostly boiled off.

Regular readers of *RockRecipes.com* are probably tiring of me forever stating the obvious. You simply cannot have enough great side dish recipes in your culinary arsenal. Great side dishes can elevate any meal and make it more enjoyable.

Of course, Spouse is still the Soup Queen and a few of her new favourites obviously had to make the cut for this book. Her Homemade Tomato Soup is now a family classic in our home.

This time around, I've expanded this category to include a sandwich. My Turkey Waldorf Salad Sandwich Wraps are the perfect collision of salad and sandwich.

side dishes, soups, sandwiches & salads

Lemon Mint Orzo Salad

PREP TIME **15** MINUTES | COOK TIME **10** MINUTES | SERVES **6**

At summer's end there's still plenty of fresh mint in the small herb garden growing a few steps from my back door. It is one of the hardiest and fastest-growing herbs you can cultivate and makes a fresh addition to this bright pasta salad.

This is an incredibly versatile recipe. Substitute practically any small pasta and serve alongside lunch or as a summer barbecue side dish.

---

1 cup **uncooked orzo** (use 1½-2 cups for larger pastas)

½ small **red pepper**, diced small

⅓ cup **extra-virgin olive oil**

2 tbsp **honey**

juice of ½ large **lemon**

3 tbsp **fresh mint**, chopped

1 tsp **lemon zest**, finely grated

pinch **salt** and **pepper** to season

1. Cook the pasta in salted water until tender but not mushy. Drain and rinse with cold water. Let stand for 10 minutes to drain completely.

2. Add the pasta to a bowl, along with the diced red pepper.

3. To make the dressing, whisk together the olive oil, honey, lemon juice, mint, lemon zest, salt, and pepper.

4. Pour the dressing over the pasta and peppers and toss together well. Refrigerate for an hour before serving, tossing the pasta salad at least a couple of times during the chilling time.

Spinach Parmesan Quinoa

PREP TIME 10 MINUTES | **COOK TIME 20 MINUTES** | **SERVES 6**

1½ cups **water**

1 cup **quinoa**

½ tsp **salt**

3 tbsp **olive oil**

2 cloves **garlic**, minced

1 small **shallot**, minced

1 small **red, yellow,** or **orange bell pepper,** diced

1 small **deseeded tomato**, diced

½ cup **pitted olives** (optional)

½ tsp **black pepper**

2 cups **fresh baby spinach leaves**

¼ cup **Parmesan cheese,** grated

olive oil and shards of **Parmesan**, for garnish

A delicious, healthy side dish that goes with everything from grilled chicken and fish to baked pork chops.

Finished with a drizzle of olive oil and shards of Parmesan, this would also make a terrific vegetarian lunch idea or part of a Meatless Monday supper.

---

1. Bring the water, quinoa, and ½ tsp of salt to a boil over low heat. Cover and simmer very slowly for 15 to 20 minutes until the grains are cooked but still a little firm to the bite. As in cooking rice, I like to keep the pot covered tightly, turn off the burner in the last 5 minutes and let it sit, then fluff with a fork when it's done.

2. In a wok or large sauté pan, sauté the garlic and shallot in the olive oil to soften, but do not let it brown.

3. Add the diced bell pepper and tomato, the olives and the black pepper. Sauté for only 1 minute to heat the peppers through.

4. Remove from the heat and toss in the cooked quinoa, spinach, and Parmesan cheese.

5. Toss together well until the spinach wilts, and serve immediately with a drizzle of extra virgin olive oil and shards of Parmesan as a garnish.

Deviled Egg Potato Salad

PREP TIME **15** MINUTES | COOK TIME **20** MINUTES | SERVES **8** OR MORE

Potato salad is one of those things I like to make a day in advance. I think it tastes better when the flavours have been allowed to sit for a while. I especially like potato salad to be very cold, and the convenience of pulling it from the fridge when you're ready to serve is unparalleled.

A cross between a favourite potato salad and a deviled egg recipe, the flavours are very simple and satisfying, but what made this dish for me is the chopped sweet pickles. Their tart, crunchy sweetness is amazingly delicious in this salad.

---

6 cups **potatoes**, cooked, cut in small chunks or diced (about 10-12 medium-sized potatoes)

6 **eggs**, hard-boiled

¾ cup **plain mayonnaise** (not salad dressing or salad cream)

½ cup **sweet pickles, roughly chopped**

¼ cup **sweet pickle juice**

2 tbsp **whole grain Dijon mustard**

1 tbsp **honey**

½ tsp **black pepper,** coarsely ground

½ tsp **salt**

½ tsp **turmeric**

1. Cook the potatoes in salted water and let them cool completely, or at least until they are cool enough to handle. Chop them into small chunks or about a ½-inch dice.

2. Hard boil the eggs for about 10-12 minutes. Drain off the boiling water, cover the eggs in cold water, and let them cool for 10-15 minutes before peeling off the shells. Cut the eggs in half and remove the yolks to a small bowl. Chop the egg whites into small pieces and add to the chopped potatoes.

3. Add about 1 tbsp of the mayo to the egg yolks and mash with a fork until the yolks and mayo form a smooth paste.

4. Add the mashed egg yolks to the chopped potatoes along with all of the remaining ingredients.

5. Toss together well until all of the potatoes are evenly coated in the dressing that forms.

6. Cover and chill the potato salad for several hours or overnight before serving.

Summer Corn Soup *with* Grilled Shrimp Sriracha Salsa

PREP TIME **15** MINUTES | COOK TIME **15** MINUTES | SERVES **4-6**

FOR THE CORN SOUP

1 small **onion**, chopped fine

2 cloves **garlic**, chopped

2 tbsp **olive oil**

3½ cups **fresh corn kernels** (or frozen if fresh is unavailable)

3 cups **vegetable stock** or chicken stock

½ tsp **dried thyme**

½ tsp **pepper**

½ tsp **salt**

1 cup **milk** (or try undiluted 2% evaporated milk for extra richness)

FOR THE GRILLED SHRIMP SALSA

12 large **shrimp**

1 small **red onion**, cut in chunks

1 small **bell pepper**, cut in chunks

1 tsp **vegetable oil** (approximately)

salt and **pepper** to season

2 tbsp **chives**, chopped

2 tsp **sriracha sauce**, more or less to taste

This is a fantastic starter course for when sweet corn season comes around. However, you can easily use frozen sweet corn whenever fresh is not available; it will still be delicious.

The slightly charred, smokey flavours of the grilled shrimp salsa are incredibly complementary with the sweet soup and provide great textural difference, making the soup a satisfying summer lunch option, too.

TO MAKE THE CORN SOUP

1. In a small saucepan over medium-low heat, slowly sauté the onion and garlic in the olive oil until the onions have softened but not browned.

2. Add the corn, vegetable stock, thyme, pepper, and salt, and bring to a slow simmer.

3. Simmer for 15 minutes, then purée the soup in a blender. When smooth, pour in the milk and blend well.

4. Return the soup to the pot and simmer for only a couple of minutes more. Taste the soup and give it a final seasoning of salt and pepper if needed before serving with the grilled shrimp salsa added to the centre of the bowls.

TO MAKE THE GRILLED SHRIMP PASTA

1. Use metal skewers if you can, but if you are using bamboo skewers, soak them in water for about 1 hour before use.

2. Add alternating pieces of shrimp, onion, and pepper to the skewers. Brush the shrimp and vegetables lightly on both sides with the vegetable oil before seasoning with salt and pepper.

3. Add the skewers to a very hot, preheated grill and cook for about 1½-2 minutes per side depending on the size of the shrimp you use.

4. Remove the shrimp and vegetables from the skewers and chop them into small pieces.

5. Toss the chopped shrimp and vegetables with the chopped chives and sriracha sauce before serving with the soup.

Homemade Tomato Soup

PREP TIME **15** MINUTES | COOK TIME **30** MINUTES | SERVES **8** OR MORE

This is a homemade comfort food classic you'll love.

It's quick and easy to make, using good quality canned tomatoes. The little bit of effort that is required for a homemade tomato soup pays off big in terms of flavour and a little extra comfort food joy, especially on a chilly winter afternoon.

This soup makes an ideal warm and comforting lunch accompanied by a perfectly crispy and gooey grilled cheese sandwich.

---

3 tbsp **olive oil**

1 large **white onion**, diced small

4 cloves **garlic**, minced

2 cans (28 oz) diced or puréed **tomatoes** (7 cups total; San Marzano tomatoes are best)

2 cups **vegetable stock** (low or no sodium added)

2 tbsp **honey**

3 **bay leaves**

1½ tsp **dried oregano**

½ tsp **white pepper** (or up to 1 tsp, to taste)

salt to season

1. Add the olive oil, onion, and garlic to a Dutch oven or large saucepan and sauté over medium-low heat until the onions have fully cooked and softened.

2. Add the rest of the ingredients and simmer for 30-40 minutes, stirring often.

3. Remove the bay leaves and purée with an immersion blender until smooth. You can also use a regular blender, doing the soup in 2 or 3 batches as necessary. Be sure that the lid to the blender is vented or pressure can build up inside and the cover will blow off, creating a very messy kitchen. Not that that's ever happened to me.

Chicken, Thyme, and Lentil Soup

PREP TIME **15** MINUTES | COOK TIME **45** MINUTES | SERVES **6**

4 tbsp **olive oil**

1½ cups **carrots**, diced

1 cup **parsnip**, diced

1 medium **red onion**

3 cloves **garlic**

1 tsp **salt**

½ tsp **black pepper**

6-8 cups low-sodium **chicken stock**

½ cup **green lentils**

4-6 sprigs **fresh thyme**

2 **bay leaves**

2-3 cups leftover **grilled** or **roasted chicken**, diced

salt and **pepper** to season

Spouse is still the Soup Queen and still makes dozens of different comforting soups.

This one is a hearty and healthy soup that makes the most of leftover roast chicken or turkey. It is a simple and comforting meal, and if you have homemade chicken stock, it really adds a special touch.

1. Heat olive oil in a large saucepan. Add the carrots, parsnip, onions, garlic, salt, and pepper and sauté together until the onions begin to soften.

2. Add the chicken stock, lentils, thyme, and bay leaves.

3. Simmer for about 20 minutes or until the lentils are almost cooked.

4. Add the cooked chicken and taste, seasoning with salt and pepper if necessary.

5. Simmer for only an additional 10 minutes before serving.

tip > I'm always sure to save the bones after I roast a chicken to make my own stock in the oven. This recipe is a testament to no food wasted, using all the delicious parts of a chicken and stretching it into two satisfying meals.

Garlic Butter Biscuits

PREP TIME 20 MINUTES | **COOK TIME 20 MINUTES** | **SERVES 8-10 LARGE BISCUITS**

If you're a garlic lover like me, this is a recipe you really must try. These biscuits are such a versatile side, great alongside soup or a hearty chili, Southern fried chicken, or an indulgent steak dinner. They make the base of excellent breakfast sandwiches, too!

However you choose to eat them, these biscuits are a welcome addition to many tasty meals.

FOR THE GARLIC BUTTER

½ cup **soft butter**

3-4 cloves **garlic**, minced

FOR THE BISCUIT DOUGH

2¼ cups **all-purpose flour**

3 tsp **baking powder**

½ cup **garlic butter** (prepared earlier as directed)

1 cup **buttermilk**

note > As a substitute for buttermilk, just stir 1 tbsp of plain vinegar or lemon juice into regular milk to sour it.

TO MAKE THE GARLIC BUTTER

note > Do this an hour or more in advance; even the day before is perfectly fine. This garlic butter will easily keep for a week in the fridge.

1. Heat 3 tbsp of the butter over low heat. You do not want the butter to brown at all.

2. Add the garlic and sauté for just 1 minute or so until it softens.

3. Remove from heat and allow to cool almost to room temperature.

4. Stir it into the remainder of the ½ cup of soft butter at room temperature until thoroughly combined.

5. Spoon the garlic butter onto a piece of plastic wrap and wrap it loosely before gently forming it into a small log shape.

6. Refrigerate the butter until firm, then chop into small pieces about the size of the top of your thumb.

TO MAKE THE BISCUIT DOUGH

1. Preheat the oven to 375°F.

2. In a food processor, blend together the flour and baking powder.

3. Pulse in the very cold garlic butter pieces. Do not over-incorporate the butter into the flour. Similar to making a flaky pastry, small pieces of butter should be visible in the flour.

4. Transfer this mixture from the food processor into a large mixing bowl and make a well in the centre. Pour in the buttermilk.

5. Working very quickly with a wooden spoon, fold the dry mixture through the buttermilk, only until the flour disappears, then stop immediately.

6. Drop the sticky dough onto a well-floured countertop or breadboard. Sprinkle the top of the dough with additional flour as well as flouring your hands to handle the dough. I don't even use a rolling pin for these biscuits, the dough is soft enough to pat it out gently with floured hands to a thickness of about 1½ inches.

7. Using a sharp 3-inch biscuit cutter, cut the biscuits out and place them on a parchment paper-lined baking sheet. I recommend aluminum baking sheets because they tolerate the higher oven temperature without burning the bottom of the biscuits.

8. Bake for about 20 minutes or until the tops of the biscuits are evenly golden brown.

Smash Roasted Potatoes

PREP TIME **10** MINUTES | COOK TIME **1 HOUR** | SERVES **4-6**

Fantastic potato recipes are one thing you cannot have enough of. These crispy smashed potatoes roasted in their skins became a favourite of my kids.

This versatile recipe can be made to suit whatever main dishes with which you are serving them. Try roasting with a few cloves of garlic and rosemary, add sage or summer savoury, or thyme and a squeeze of lemon. However you fancy them, these potatoes are sure to be a hit.

2-3 lbs **white** or **yellow potatoes**

6 tbsp **olive oil**, approximately

kosher salt and **pepper** to season

cloves of **garlic** and **fresh herbs** of your choice (optional)

1. Choose potatoes of a similar size so that they cook evenly in the same amount of time and scrub them well.

2. Boil the whole potatoes in salted water until a fork inserts into them easily but they are not falling apart, about 15-20 minutes depending on their size.

3. Strain the potatoes and place them on a hard surface like a wooden cutting board.

> **tip** > Some people use a flat potato masher to flatten the potatoes, but I use a large can of tomatoes to get a perfectly flat surface that tends to stay together more. Whatever you use, the key is to apply slow, even, gentle pressure until the potato just breaks open. You want to try and get them to an even thickness.

5. I like to use glass baking dishes for these because I find they get the potatoes crispier. You may need to use a couple of pans because you do not want to crowd the pan or have the potatoes touching at all. They need just a little space between them in order to get crispy. I use two 9x9-inch glass baking dishes.

6. Preheat the oven to 400°F.

7. Brush the bottom of the pan(s) with half of the olive oil. If using two pans, you may need a little more oil.

8. Add the flattened potatoes to the pans so that they are not touching each other and season them with a little kosher salt and pepper before drizzling them with the remaining olive oil.

9. Pop them into the hot oven for about 45 minutes, turning them halfway through the cooking time. You may find some potato varieties take a little longer, depending upon moisture content. Whenever they are browned and crispy, they are ready.

Turkey Waldorf Salad Sandwich Wraps

PREP TIME **15 MINUTES** | SERVES **4 WRAPS**

A leftover turkey sandwich will never be the same once you sample this delicious combination of flavours and textures. Plus it's just as good using leftover roast chicken, if you like.

This wrap sandwich was inspired by a classic Waldorf Salad, which has toasted walnuts, apples, grapes, and celery.

These are a fresh and satisfying choice for lunch or to pack for a picnic. I love the idea of tying the parchment paper with butcher string before you cut into the wrapper. It makes for a very appealing, nostalgic presentation.

¼ cup **toasted pecans**

¼ cup **low fat mayo**

1 tbsp **lemon juice**

¼ tsp **paprika** or **smoked paprika**

pinch **dried summer savoury** or **sage**

salt and **pepper** to season

2 cups diced **turkey breast**

½ cup **seedless grapes**, cut in half

¼ cup **celery**, finely diced

¼ cup **red pepper**, finely diced

3 tbsp **dried cranberries**

4 large **flour tortillas**, white or whole wheat

romaine lettuce or **spinach**

1. Toast the pecans in a shallow pan at 350°F for 10 minutes, tossing once at the 5-minute mark. Set aside to cool.

2. Stir together the mayo, lemon juice, paprika, savoury, salt, and pepper to form a dressing.

3. Place the turkey, grapes, celery, red pepper, dried cranberries, and toasted pecans in a bowl.

4. Pour the dressing on and toss well.

5. Cut four 12-inch squares or larger of parchment paper and lay a tortilla on top of each one.

6. Add a few layers of lettuce leaves or spinach, about 5 inches wide from the centre of the tortilla.

7. Spoon the turkey salad on top of the lettuce.

8. Bring the 2 sides up over the salad a little so that they form the ends of the sandwich wrap. then roll the tortilla as you would for a burrito.

9. Roll the sandwich wrap in the parchment paper, bringing 2 sides of the paper over the ends of the wrap in the same way that you rolled the sandwich.

10. Tie butcher string about 1½ inches from each end.

11. Store the wraps in the fridge until ready to serve. When serving, use a sharp serrated knife to cut straight through the paper and wrap at once.

Garlic Thyme Fondant Potato

PREP TIME **20** MINUTES | COOK TIME **40** MINUTES | SERVES **8** OR MORE

Fondant potatoes may seem to some like a very dated recipe, and indeed it was at a "fancy" restaurant back in the eighties where I first tasted them. I believe, though, that delicious never really goes out of style.

It is the mix of tastes and textures that makes these potatoes so special. The butter and stock add richness and help to give their characteristic golden colour. The garlic and thyme also bring fantastic complementary flavours to the dish.

---

8   medium-sized **russet potatoes**

4   tbsp **butter**

2   tbsp **olive oil**

salt and **pepper** to season

3   cloves **garlic**, sliced

3   sprigs **fresh thyme**

1½ cups (approximately) **low sodium chicken stock**, boiling hot

2   additional tbsp **butter**

1. First, choose a pan that's the right size for the potatoes. I mostly use a 9x9-inch glass pan and peel and chop the perfect amount of potatoes that will fit into it. Once you've determined that, remove the potatoes and heat the baking dish in a 400°F oven while you brown the potatoes.

2. Peel the potatoes and cut them into about 2-inch thick cylinders. Cut off the rounded ends and try to keep all the potato pieces the same size.

3. Heat the butter and olive oil over medium heat in a cast iron skillet or non-stick sauté pan. Add the sliced garlic and sprigs of thyme. Cook for just a minute or so to soften the garlic, then remove it from the pan along with the thyme. Set the garlic and thyme aside for later.

4. Season the potatoes on both sides with salt and pepper, and brown both ends of the potatoes in the garlic thyme butter and oil mixture until golden, about 3-4 minutes or so per side over medium-high heat.

5. While you are browning the potatoes, heat the chicken stock to boiling.

note > You can simmer this jus in a small saucepan to reduce it even further, if you like, and intensify its flavour.

tip > I like to serve the roasting liquid for the fondant potatoes on the side to pour over them like a jus.

6. Remove the browned potatoes from the cast iron pan and fit them into the heated baking dish. Tuck the garlic slices and thyme sprigs used to flavour the oil and butter between the potatoes. Pour on the hot chicken stock just until the potatoes are half submerged.

7. Dot the top of each potato with a little bit of butter, then return the pan to the oven for about 30 minutes or until the potatoes are fork tender. Serve immediately.

Alfredo Mac and Cheese

PREP TIME **20** MINUTES | COOK TIME **1** HOUR | SERVES **8**

A good version of pasta alfredo has always been one of my favourite dishes. The uncomplicated but rich creamy sauce, flavoured simply with garlic and Parmesan cheese and perfectly coating al dente pasta is a classic for a reason.

Mac and cheese is a kid favourite at our house, and we like to make many versions, which is where the inspiration for this glorious recipe came from. The rich, creamy flavour of a pasta alfredo is an indulgent addition to a traditional, baked mac and cheese.

tip > Rotini is great for this recipe because its shape holds the maximum amount of sauce.

4	cups cooked **rotini** (or 3 cups if using a smaller-sized pasta like macaroni or fusilli)
1½	cups **heavy cream** (whipping cream, 35%)
1½	cups **milk**
3	tbsp **butter**
2	tbsp **flour**
¼	tsp **white pepper**
3	cloves **garlic**, minced
¾	cup **Parmesan cheese**, finely grated
12	oz part **skim mozzarella cheese**, grated

1. Boil the pasta in salted water just to al dente. You almost want to undercook the pasta a little at this stage because it will continue to cook in the oven later. Drain the pasta very well. You can toss it in 1 tsp of butter to prevent it sticking together, if you like.

2. Preheat the oven to 350°F and lightly grease an 8- to 10-cup baking dish with butter.

3. Combine the cream and milk and scald them almost to the boiling point in a small saucepan or in the microwave oven. It is important for the liquid to be very hot so that the sauce will thicken quickly.

4. In a medium-sized saucepan, melt the butter over medium-low heat and add the flour and white pepper.

5. Cook together until it starts to get foamy, then add the garlic and stir for only 30 seconds or so. You don't want to brown the garlic at all, just soften it a little.

6. Whisking constantly, slowly pour in scalded cream and milk in 3 portions. When the sauce shows signs of thickening, quickly add the next portion. When the last portion has been added, continue to cook for 2 more minutes, stirring constantly. The sauce will be a thin white sauce at this stage.

7. A little at a time, sprinkle in the finely grated Parmesan cheese, whisking constantly until all the cheese has melted and the sauce is smooth.

8. Add half of the cooked pasta to the greased dish. Pour on half of the sauce and sprinkle with half of the mozzarella cheese. Repeat the layers of pasta and sauce and sprinkle the remaining mozzarella on top.

9. Bake for 45-60 minutes or until the sauce is bubbling and the top just starts to lightly brown.

10. Serve as a great side dish or with a simple mixed salad as a complete meal.

A weekend brunch in our family has become just as important as Sunday dinner. We try to manage both in a single weekend if we can, but if dinner isn't possible, it's worth the effort to rise a little early and prepare a memorable meal for the family.

One of the things I love about writing my blog is the great feedback I get from brunch junkies like me. For many it has become a new weekend entertaining tradition, just like at our house.

I'll guarantee if you start your own weekend brunch tradition, there will be no shortage of willing guests to accept an invitation.

brunch

Buttermilk Biscuit Cinnamon Rolls

PREP TIME **20 MINUTES** | COOK TIME **25 MINUTES** | SERVES **8 ROLLS**

As a die-hard cinnamon roll lover, I was a bit skeptical of trying a recipe without a yeast-raised dough. However, this is a quicker version using a homemade buttermilk biscuit.

The first time I baked them, I sat with my morning coffee, enjoying one warm from the oven. I realized I did not miss spending all that time waiting to enjoy a great cinnamon roll at all.

Plenty of other folks must have thought the same, because the recipe was an instant hit on my blog. It's definitely one to try for your next weekend brunch.

---

2 cups all-purpose flour

¼ cup sugar

4 tsp baking powder

¼ tsp baking soda

¼ cup + 1 tbsp very cold salted butter, cut in small cubes

1 cup buttermilk

2 tsp vanilla extract

½ cup brown sugar

3 tbsp melted butter

2 tsp ground cinnamon

¾ cup raisins (optional)

FOR THE VANILLA GLAZE (OPTIONAL)

¾ cup icing sugar (powdered sugar)

3 tbsp milk

1 tbsp melted butter

¼ tsp vanilla extract

1. Preheat the oven to 375°F.

2. In a food processor, blend together the flour, sugar, baking powder, and baking soda.

3. Pulse in the butter. Do not over-incorporate the butter into the flour. Similar to making a flaky pastry, small pieces of butter should be visible in the flour.

4. Transfer this mixture from the food processor into a large mixing bowl and make a well in the centre. Pour in the buttermilk and vanilla extract.

5. Working very quickly with a wooden spoon, fold the dry mixture through the buttermilk, only until the flour disappears, then stop immediately.

6. Drop the sticky dough onto a well-floured countertop or bread board. Sprinkle the top of the dough with additional flour as well as flouring your hands to handle the dough.

TO MAKE THE ROLLS

1. Roll out the dough into a rectangle about 9x18 inches.

2. Mix together the brown sugar, melted butter, and cinnamon into a paste.

3. Spread this paste evenly onto the rolled dough using a rubber spatula. Sprinkle the surface of the dough with the raisins if you choose to use them.

4. Press the raisins down into the dough gently with the palm of your hand. This helps hold them in place as you roll.

5. Starting at the shorter end of the dough, roll the dough up tightly and pinch the end of the dough together to seal the end into the roll.

6. Slice the roll into 8 equally thick slices and place on a parchment paper-lined baking sheet, a couple of inches apart. I recommend aluminum baking sheets because they tolerate the higher oven temperature without burning the bottom of the biscuits.

note > You can brush the rolls with an egg wash to help them brown and sprinkle the tops with turbinado sugar for a little crunch if you like.

For an egg wash, simply whisk together one egg with a tablespoon of water and brush lightly on top of the unbaked rolls. You will NOT need all of the egg wash; in fact, you won't need much of it.

7. Bake in the preheated oven for about 20-25 minutes or until the tops of the biscuits are evenly golden brown.

8. Drizzle with vanilla glaze if you like.

TO MAKE THE VANILLA GLAZE

1. Mix together all ingredients until smooth. You can add a little more icing sugar or milk to make the glaze thicker or thinner in consistency to suit your taste.

Guacamole Eggs Benedict

PREP TIME **20 MINUTES** | COOK TIME **5 MINUTES** | SERVES **4**

4   slices of crusty bread, toasted

4-8 eggs, poached (over-easy or scrambled are fine too, if you prefer)

8   slices bacon, crisp-cooked and roughly chopped

FOR THE GUACAMOLE

1   large ripe avocado, or 2 small

1   clove garlic, finely minced

juice of ½ small lemon

2   tbsp hot sauce, or to taste (optional)

½   tsp lemon zest, finely chopped

½   tsp fresh black pepper

¼   tsp sea salt, or to taste

FOR THE SALSA

2   medium tomatoes, deseeded, diced small (I use one red and one yellow for good colour)

¼   cup red onion, finely minced

1   small jalapeno pepper, deseeded and finely minced

1   clove garlic, minced

1   tbsp lemon juice (a small squeeze)

salt and pepper to season

Eggs Benedict is one of my longtime brunch indulgences. I can't seem to resist it on any breakfast menu.

I also love making different, delicious twists on the classic dish, using everything from potato latkes, toutons, and even crab cakes or fish cakes.

This is a bit of a healthier version of eggs Benedict, served with creamy guacamole and a fresh and spicy tomato jalapeno salsa. It's incredibly satisfying as a casual weekend brunch, and easy enough to dress up to serve a crowd when entertaining guests.

---

note > It's important to have all your ingredients at room temperature for the guacamole and salsa so that they don't cool down the eggs and toast and make the entire dish too cold to enjoy. Leave the ingredients out on the counter overnight if you plan to make this in the morning.

TO MAKE THE GUACAMOLE

1. Crush the avocado roughly in a mortar and pestle, or just mash with a fork.

2. Add the remaining ingredients and stir well.

3. Store in a glass bowl with plastic wrap touching the surface of the guacamole to preserve the colour.

TO MAKE THE SALSA

1. Simply toss all of the ingredients together in a glass or plastic bowl.

to assemble the dish >

1. Spread guacamole over the toasted, crusty bread. Place an egg or two on top, and sprinkle with the bacon pieces. Finally, top with the fresh salsa and serve.

Bakery Style Blueberry Muffins

PREP TIME **15 MINUTES** | COOK TIME **35 MINUTES**
SERVES **6 JUMBO MUFFINS** OR **12 REGULAR MUFFINS**

Is bigger always better? When it comes to muffins, I definitely think it is. I use a jumbo muffin pan to achieve a good crunchy muffin top that breaks free of the limitations of the height of the pan. No worries though, these are still darn delicious when made in a standard muffin pan.

These are big, moist, perfectly baked blueberry muffins with a distinct, crispy-edged muffin top. Just like your favourite bakery muffins!

3	cups flour
3	tsp baking powder
¼	tsp salt
2	eggs
1¼	cups sugar
2	tsp vanilla extract
¼	cup butter, melted
¼	cup vegetable oil
1	cup evaporated milk, straight from the can
2	tbsp apple cider vinegar, or lemon juice
2	cups blueberries, fresh or frozen (see notes for tips on using frozen)

1. Preheat the oven to 350°F. Grease a jumbo muffin pan (6 muffin size) with butter, including the top of the pan.

2. Sift together the flour, baking powder, and salt, and set aside.

3. In the bowl of a stand mixer with the whisk attachment in place, whisk together the eggs, sugar, and vanilla extract on high speed until foamy and slightly stiffened.

4. Mix together the melted butter and vegetable oil in a measuring cup with a spout.

5. Slowly add the oil and butter mixture to the egg mixture in a slow stream as the mixer continues to whisk.

6. Place the 2 tbsp of apple cider vinegar in a measuring cup and fill to the one cup mark with the evaporated milk.

7. Add this soured milk slowly to the mixing bowl, continuing to mix but at a reduced speed.

8. Fold in the dry ingredients by hand with a rubber spatula, being careful not to over-mix. Don't worry about lumps in the batter, they are fine. When the dry ingredients are almost incorporated, gently fold in the blueberries.

9. Spoon batter into the well-greased jumbo muffin tins, filling them to the top. If you like, you can sprinkle about 1 tsp each of blueberries and turbinado sugar over the top of each muffin before baking.

tip > You can bake these in standard muffin pans. Just increase the heat to 375 or 400°F and bake for about 20 minutes or until a toothpick inserted into the centre comes out clean.

10. Bake for about 35-40 minutes or until a wooden toothpick inserted into the centre of a muffin comes out clean.

note > I have had a couple of questions on *RockRecipes.com* about using frozen blueberries. Yes, they are fine to use, but you may find the baking time to be a bit longer. Watch the muffins carefully and trust the toothpick test to know when they are perfectly baked.

Parmesan Spinach Quiche

PREP TIME **10 MINUTES** | COOK TIME **30 MINUTES** | SERVES **4**

This shortcut recipe uses ready-made frozen puff pastry, making it easy to get into the oven in mere minutes. The quick tomato and garlic compote comes together in a small sauté pan in just a few minutes while the quiche bakes.

The result is an easy and elegant recipe versatile enough for a weekend brunch. If, like me, you're a fan of breakfast for dinner, this recipe fits that bill perfectly too.

FOR THE QUICHE

- 1 lb sheet of frozen puff pastry (about 10- to 12-inch square, or half the package)
- 8 eggs
- ⅓ cup Parmesan cheese, finely grated
- ⅓ cup milk or whipping cream
- pinch salt
- pepper to season
- 1 cup fresh spinach, chopped (you can use frozen, but squeeze out any excess liquid before chopping)

FOR THE TOMATO GARLIC COMPOTE

- 1 tbsp olive oil
- 2 cloves fresh garlic, minced
- 4 tomatoes, diced large
- salt and pepper to season
- ½ tsp honey

TO MAKE THE QUICHE

1. Preheat the oven to 375°F.

2. Lightly grease an 8x8-inch baking dish. Place the pastry into the dish so that it goes evenly up all sides.

3. Whisk together the eggs, Parmesan cheese, milk, salt, and pepper.

4. Stir in the spinach and pour into the prepared pastry. Bake for 30-40 minutes or until the pastry is golden brown and the centre of the quiche is firm. Serve immediately with the warm tomato garlic compote.

TO MAKE THE TOMATO GARLIC COMPOTE

1. Heat the olive oil over medium heat in a small sauté pan.

2. Add the garlic and sauté for only 1 minute or less to soften but not brown the garlic.

3. Add the diced tomatoes, salt, and pepper.

4. Sauté together for a few minutes until enough liquid reduces off to give the compote a thick, chunky consistency. In the last minute or so, add the honey. Serve warm over the baked quiche.

Ultimate Bran Muffins

PREP TIME **15 MINUTES** | COOK TIME **20 MINUTES** | SERVES **12**

The best bakery bran muffins I've tasted always had a lingering, slight background flavour of molasses. I think that element is essential, plus not overdoing it on the oil.

This hearty recipe has just the right texture, flavour, and moistness without being too oily. It's a perfect breakfast muffin, but great to take along for a brunch or office coffee break, too.

1½ cups bran cereal (All-Bran, or bran flakes crushed to make 1½ cups)

1⅔ cups milk

2 cups all-purpose flour

3 tsp baking powder

½ tsp salt

½ cup brown sugar

⅓ cup molasses

⅓ cup canola oil (or other vegetable oil)

¼ cup butter, melted

2 eggs

¾ cup raisins (optional—plus extra to garnish tops before baking, if you like)

1. Begin by soaking the bran cereal in the milk for 10-15 minutes.

2. Preheat the oven to 400°F. Grease a 12-muffin pan generously, including the top of the pan. If using paper muffin liners, it's still a good idea to grease the top of the pan to prevent sticking.

3. Combine the flour, baking powder, and salt.

4. In a large bowl, whisk together the brown sugar, molasses, oil, melted butter, and eggs until well blended.

5. Stir in the bran and milk mixture.

6. Fold in the dry ingredients until the batter is smooth.

7. If you are using them, add the raisins during the last few turns of folding in the flour mixture.

8. Spoon the batter evenly into the prepared muffin pan.

9. Bake for about 20 minutes or until a wooden toothpick inserted into the centre of the muffins comes out clean. Cool for 5 minutes in the pan before transferring the muffins to a wire rack to cool.

Southern Sausage Gravy

PREP TIME **15 MINUTES** | COOK TIME **15 MINUTES** | SERVES **6**

Having travelled extensively throughout the southern states, I can tell you that I've eaten my fair share of biscuits and gravy. It has been the star of many a roadside diner breakfast for me on many occasions. (And the cause of disappointment in a few too, if I'm honest.)

I decided to try my own spin on a sausage gravy that does not rely on heavy cream or whole milk. I also wanted a more intensely flavoured, less-milky gravy than some of the traditional gravy I've seen.

You can turn any kind of sausage into a delicious comfort food breakfast or brunch when served with flaky biscuits.

---

1 lb sausage meat (removed from casings if necessary)

4 tbsp butter

½ cup onion, chopped

2 cloves garlic, chopped

4 tbsp all-purpose flour

1½ cups chicken stock (sodium-free or low sodium, preferably; see notes below)

1½ cups milk (I use 2%)

½ tsp black pepper

salt to season

pinch of chili flakes (optional, or to taste)

1. Start by breaking up the sausage meat into small pieces and brown it well over medium to medium-high heat. You want to get some good colour when browning the sausage, to add extra flavour to the gravy.

2. When the sausage is cooked, remove it from the pan and set aside.

3. Turn the pan down to medium or medium-low and melt the butter.

4. Add the onions and garlic and cook for only 1 minute or so to begin softening the onions.

5. Add the flour to the pan and mix it in well. Cook for 1 minute until foamy.

notes >

Heating the combination of milk and stock (or all milk, if you prefer) to scalding in the microwave or in a pot on the stovetop will speed up the cooking time of the gravy.

You can also "double reduce" the stock before using it, to intensify the flavour of the gravy. I often do this for any gravy using stock. Basically, take double the amount of stock in the recipe and simmer it until the volume reduces by half. This will make the stock twice as intense, for a richer gravy with more depth of flavour.

6.   Combine the chicken stock and milk (or use all milk, if you prefer) and add to the pan along with the black pepper. Don't add salt yet.

7.   Turn the pan to low and simmer slowly for 5 minutes or so, stirring often, until the gravy thickens.

note > Taste the gravy to see if it needs additional salt. Depending on the type of sausage you use, there may be enough salt in it to season the gravy properly. I recommend low-sodium chicken stock, but if you're using regular, this will also add salt to the dish. In any case, seasoning at the end is the best way to not over-season the gravy.

8.   Serve over warm biscuits.

Lemon Cranberry Scones

PREP TIME **15 MINUTES** | COOK TIME **15 MINUTES** | SERVES **18 SMALL SCONES OR 8 LARGE**

Enjoy fragrant lemon and tart cranberry in every bite of these soft and tender scones, finished with an easy-to-make lemon glaze. These elegant, impressive little scones are perfect for afternoon tea or weekend brunch. I like to make the smaller scones if serving them for afternoon tea and the larger scones if packing them into lunches or for picnics.

FOR THE SCONES

1⅔ cups all-purpose flour

3 tbsp white sugar

2½ tsp baking powder

zest of 1 large lemon, finely grated

pinch table salt

3 tbsp butter

½ cup milk

1 egg

½ tsp vanilla extract (optional)

¾ cup dried cranberries (see note)

FOR THE EASY LEMON GLAZE

⅔ cup icing sugar (powdered sugar)

1 tbsp lemon juice, approximately

zest of ½ lemon, finely grated

1. Preheat the oven to 400°F.

2. In a food processor add the flour, sugar, baking powder, lemon zest, and salt. Pulse to mix together well. (You can just mix the ingredients in a bowl if you prefer the manual method.)

3. Pulse in the butter until the mixture resembles a coarse meal (or just use your fingertips to rub the butter through the dry ingredients until the same texture is achieved).

4. Whisk together the milk, egg, and vanilla. Reserve a few teaspoons of the liquid to brush on top of the scones. This helps them brown nicely.

5. Add the liquid to the dry ingredients along with the dried cranberries and stir in quickly with a wooden spoon until it forms a soft dough. It should be a little sticky. Don't overwork the dough or your scones will not rise well and will have a less tender texture.

6. Turn the dough out onto a well-floured board or countertop.

7. Lightly sprinkle the top of the dough with flour, and just using your hands, form the dough into a round, about ¾-inch thick.

8. Using a 1½-inch biscuit cutter, cut out your scones and place them about 2 inches apart on a parchment-lined baking sheet.

note > I use dried cranberries in these scones, but you could use fresh cranberries chopped in raisin-sized pieces. One thing about dried cranberries is they seem to vary greatly in moisture content by brand. I also find them to be far more dehydrated when I buy them at the bulk store. If your dried cranberries are not soft and pliable like raisins, I suggest rehydrating them in water for 30-60 minutes. That always does the trick for me.

tip > I like to make the glaze in a small shallow ramekin, which makes dipping the tops of the scones in the glaze quite easy.

9. Reroll the scraps and cut out the rest of the scones. Brush the tops of all the scones with the reserved milk and egg liquid.

10. Pop the scones into the hot oven for about 12-15 minutes or until the tops of the scones are evenly browned. Cool on a wire rack.

11. Serve with thick or clotted cream and your favourite jam.

TO MAKE THE EASY LEMON GLAZE

1. Simply mix together the ingredients until smooth, with no icing sugar lumps.

2. The glaze should be thick but still pourable. If it is too thick add a little more lemon juice, if it is too thin, add a little more icing sugar to bring it to the proper consistency.

3. After glazing the scones, let the glaze set on the scones for 30 minutes or so before serving.

Blueberry Almond Butter Muffins

PREP TIME **10 MINUTES** | COOK TIME **25 MINUTES** | SERVES **12**

These almond butter muffins came about, as recipes often do around here, from a fridge clean-out. I hate to throw anything out, especially food items. So, an open bottle of almond butter was the inspiration for what turned out to be some of the best muffins we ever made around here.

These are low fat, high-fibre muffins made without refined sugar, but they are so utterly moist and delicious, nobody will notice or care that they are a healthier option.

---

1 cup whole wheat flour

⅔ cup uncooked oatmeal, finely ground (see instructions)

¾ tsp baking powder

½ tsp baking soda

½ tsp fine sea salt, or table salt

1 cup low fat (2%) yogurt

½ cup almond butter (or any unsweetened nut butter, like peanut butter or cashew butter)

⅓ cup honey or agave syrup

1 egg

1 tsp vanilla extract

¼ tsp almond extract (optional)

1¼ cups fresh or frozen blueberries

1. Preheat oven to 350°F. Line a 12-muffin pan with large paper liners.

2. You can use pre-ground quick oats for this recipe, but if you only have large rolled oats on hand like I always do, pulse them in a food processor to break them up into a coarse meal.

3. Mix together the flour, oats, baking powder, baking soda, and salt. Set aside.

4. In the bowl of an electric mixer, add the yogurt, almond butter, honey, egg, vanilla extract, and almond extract.

5. Whisk at high speed for a few minutes until well combined.

6. Add the dry ingredients mixture and fold in gently by hand. Be careful not to over-mix or your muffins will not rise as much and will have a less tender texture.

7. When the flour mixture is almost incorporated, add the berries and fold in just until they are evenly dispersed in the batter.

8. Spoon the batter evenly into the paper-lined muffin pan. You can top them with some chopped toasted almonds and a few extra berries, if you like, to make them look even more appealing.

9. Bake for 20-25 minutes or until a toothpick inserted in the centre comes out clean. (The batch pictured took 23 minutes in my oven.)

tip > These muffins can, of course, be frozen. I like to take one, or several, from the freezer, wrap it in aluminum foil, and pop it into a 350°F oven for about 10 minutes. When reheated this way they are practically the same as fresh from the oven.

10. Cool on a wire rack for at least 10 minutes.

11. Store in an airtight container. If stored properly, I find these muffins stay moist and tender for several days.

Cheddar Ham Potato Cakes

PREP TIME **20 MINUTES** | COOK TIME **10 MINUTES** | SERVES **8 POTATO CAKES**

We've routinely been making these cakes for a while now after a baked ham dinner. Leftover baked ham pairs perfectly with mashed potatoes and pockets of melted cheddar cheese.

It's truly a leftover recipe winner, and so versatile for brunch or dinner with fried eggs on top. Add a little Hollandaise sauce with poached eggs and it's a pretty spectacular version of eggs Benny, too.

4 cups cold mashed potato

2 tbsp olive oil

½ cup onion, diced

2 cloves garlic

1½ cups ham, diced

1 cup cheddar cheese, grated (or you can dice into small cubes, as I prefer)

2 tbsp canola oil

¼ cup flour

1. If you don't already have leftover mashed potato, boil potatoes until fork tender. Mash them well without adding any butter or cream. Allow to cool to room temperature or colder (warm potatoes make the cakes more difficult to form).

2. In a small pan over medium heat, sauté the garlic and onions in the olive oil. Add to a bowl with the potatoes, ham, and cheese.

3. Form into 8 equal-sized balls and then pat them down to about 1-inch thickness.

4. Dip the cakes in flour to coat them, then place them on a parchment-paper-covered plate or tray.

5. Cover the bottom of a cast iron or non-stick frying pan with canola oil. Heat on medium for a few minutes before adding the cakes a few at a time. Don't crowd the pan or it will make it more difficult to keep the cakes intact.

6. Let them brown very well on one side before gently flipping them over to brown for an equal amount of time on the other side. Four or five minutes should do it, but the browner the better and the easier they will be to flip.

7. Transfer to a cookie sheet if making multiple batches and hold in a 200°F oven until all of the cakes are fried. Serve immediately.

Cinnamon Roll Cake

PREP TIME **20 MINUTES** | COOK TIME **45 MINUTES** | SERVES **16**

This Cinnamon Roll Cake is a variation of a simple recipe I used to make years ago in loaf pans. This version is an old-fashioned, easy to prepare, moist and delicious cake with buttery cinnamon roll flavour.

It's a favourite way to finish a brunch, easy enough to take along to the office for a coffee break treat, or even as a mid-week dessert if you find a little extra time.

FOR THE CAKE

1½ cups sugar

¾ cup butter

3 eggs

2 tsp vanilla extract

2½ cups flour

1½ tsp baking powder

½ cup whipping cream

½ cup milk (or substitute 1 cup undiluted evaporated milk for both the ½ cup whipping cream and the ½ cup milk, if you like)

FOR THE CINNAMON SWIRL

⅔ cup sugar

3 tsp cinnamon

FOR THE VANILLA GLAZE

1 cup icing sugar (powdered sugar)

2 tbsp milk

½ tsp vanilla extract

TO MAKE THE CAKE

1. Preheat oven to 350°F. Grease and flour a Bundt pan or tube pan, or line 2 small loaf pans with parchment paper.

2. Cream together the sugar and butter well.

3. Add the eggs, one at a time, beating well after each addition until light and fluffy.

4. Beat in the vanilla extract.

5. In a separate bowl, sift together the flour and baking powder.

6. Mix together the whipping cream and milk.

7. Fold the dry ingredients into the creamed mixture alternately with the milk mixture, beginning and ending with the dry ingredients. As a general rule, I add the dry ingredients in 3 portions and the milk in 2 portions.

8. In a separate bowl, stir together the additional sugar and cinnamon.

9. Divide the batter into 4 or 5 portions. Add the first portion to pan(s) and then sprinkle a few tbsp of the cinnamon sugar on top of the batter. Repeat this process until all of the batter and cinnamon sugar are used. You can sprinkle the last of the cinnamon sugar on top if there is any left.

10. Bake for 45 minutes to 1 hour, depending upon the size of your pan. Baking times vary greatly on this recipe so rely on the toothpick test to ensure that it is properly baked. When a wooden toothpick inserted in the centre comes out clean, it's done.

11. Let the cake cool in the pan(s) for 10 minutes before turning it out onto a wire rack to cool completely before glazing.

TO MAKE THE VANILLA GLAZE

1. Simply whisk the three ingredients together until smooth. The glaze should be thick but just pourable. Add a little more icing sugar or milk as needed to achieve the correct consistency.

2. Drizzle over the cooled cake. I like to use a zip-lock bag with the corner snipped off for this purpose.

Blueberry Peach Sour Cream Cake

PREP TIME **20 MINUTES** | COOK TIME **1 HOUR** | SERVES **12-16**

I created this recipe one August when I had both freshly picked Newfoundland blueberries on hand, as well as sweet, juicy peaches from the Niagara region of southern Ontario. They seemed a natural combination, so I decided to break out an old standby sour cream coffee cake recipe and top it with the summer fruits.

The result was a marriage of amazing seasonal flavours! This is a colourful and tender cake to finish a summer brunch. Don't let the season pass without trying this one!

2	cups flour
1½	tsp baking powder
¼	tsp baking soda
1⅓	cups sugar
¾	cup butter
2	tsp vanilla extract
⅔	cup sour cream
2-3	peaches, unpeeled, sliced (enough to cover the surface of the cake)
¾	cup blueberries
3-4	tbsp turbinado sugar, or demerara or brown sugar (optional)

1. Grease and flour a 9- or 10-inch springform pan and, if you like, line the bottom with parchment paper for easier release. Preheat the oven to 350°F.

2. Sift together the flour, baking powder, and baking soda and set aside.

3. Cream the sugar and butter together well. Add the vanilla extract.

4. Beat in the eggs, one at a time, beating well after each addition.

5. Fold in the dry ingredients alternately with the sour cream. I do this on low speed in my mixer. Always begin and end with the dry ingredients when adding them alternately. I generally add the dry ingredients in 3 portions and the sour cream in 2 portions.

6. Spread the batter evenly into the prepared springform pan. Arrange the peach slices so that they cover the surface, then sprinkle on the blueberries between the peach slices.

7. Sprinkle the sugar over the top of the cake and bake for approximately 1 hour. Deeper pans may take an additional 10 minutes or more. When a wooden toothpick inserted into the

centre of the cake comes out clean, it is done. When doing the toothpick test, avoid piercing the fruit, which can clean the toothpick on removal and give an inaccurate indication of whether the cake is done.

8.   Cool the cake in the pan for about 15 minutes before removing the sides of the springform pan and cooling the cake completely on a wire rack. If I'm serving it for brunch, I like to serve it warm, after at least 30 minutes out of the oven.

I published a cookies cookbook two years ago, so you might be forgiven for thinking I'd run out of new cookie recipes. But I haven't, not at all.

I am still adding brand new cookie recipes to the blog all the time, especially at the height of the holiday baking season.

None of the cookie recipes in this book appear in any previous cookbooks. They are a list of hits from the past couple of years.

From yet another two new versions in our ever-popular Nanaimo bars collection, to a treasured recipe like Old-Fashioned Cherry Bars, you're sure to find some new favourites in the pages that follow.

cookies & bars

Old-Fashioned Cherry Bars

PREP TIME **20 MINUTES** | COOK TIME **45 MINUTES** | SERVES **36 COOKIE BARS**

FOR THE BOTTOM LAYER

2 cups flour

1 cup butter

¼ cup icing sugar (powdered sugar)

FOR THE CINNAMON SWIRL

2 cups glacé cherries, cut in quarters

1½ cups brown sugar, firmly packed

1 cup pecans, chopped (optional)

1 cup dried coconut, fine cut

4 eggs

1 tsp vanilla extract

I first came across this recipe from my friend Judy Green in Ontario, who had shared a photo of these festive-looking cookies made by her neighbour, Patsy Martin. According to Judy, Patsy comes from England and was once an expert equestrian and sailor. Now in her late eighties, she is a master gardener and wonderful baker.

She also has a Newfoundland connection in that her son and his wife lived in Rocky Harbour where they worked for Parks Canada. Patsy was kind enough to share her decades-old, family-favourite, handwritten recipe with me. You can thank her for this one.

---

1. Preheat the oven to 350°F. Lightly grease a 9x13-inch baking pan and line it with parchment paper.

2. Combine the flour, butter, and icing sugar by rubbing the butter through the flour and icing sugar with your hands, until it resembles coarse crumbs. You can do this quicker and easier in a food processor, if you like.

3. Press the crumb mixture evenly into the bottom of the prepared pan.

4. Bake until the bottom crust begins to brown around the edges, about 20 minutes. Remove from the oven.

5. Mix together the remaining ingredients until well combined, and spread evenly over the bottom layer.

6. Return to the oven and bake for an additional 25-30 minutes until the top sets and gets a little golden in colour.

7. Cool completely in the pan before cutting into squares or bars.

Lime Chiffon Squares

PREP TIME **25** MINUTES | COOK TIME **APPROXIMATELY 1** HOUR | SERVES **36** SQUARES

These no-bake squares are based upon our popular Strawberry Chiffon Squares, which appear in my *Cookies* cookbook. Almost everyone in our family makes those, from aunts to siblings and cousins.

You are likely to find these in the freezer, particularly around Christmastime. My siblings and I would often get in trouble for stealing chiffon squares from the freezer as kids!

This lime version is a bright and tangy take on a family favourite recipe.

---

3 cups graham cracker crumbs

¾ cup butter, melted

4 tbsp white sugar

1 cup boiling water

2 small packages lime Jell-O

1¼ cup lime juice

300 ml sweetened condensed milk

16 oz whipping cream

8 oz mini marshmallows

zest of 3 limes

note > In Canada, sweetened condensed milk is sold in 300 ml cans. In the US, it is sold in 10 oz cans. They are actually the same size, so don't worry. One is sold by volume and the other by weight, so there is no difference.

tip > This dessert takes very little time to prepare but is best made in advance to allow the Jell-O to set, or even the day before if serving as a frozen dessert.

TO MAKE THE GRAHAM CRUMB BASE

1. Mix together the graham cracker crumbs, melted butter, and sugar.

2. Lightly grease and line a 9x13-inch baking pan with parchment paper.

3. Press the crumb mixture evenly into the prepared pan.

TO MAKE THE LIME CHIFFON LAYER

1. Combine boiling water and Jell-O, stir until dissolved.

2. Add lime juice and sweetened condensed milk.

3. Whip the cream to soft peaks, not too firm.

4. Fold marshmallows and whipped cream in to the mixture.

5. Spread over the prepared graham base and chill until the Jell-O has set.

tip > These can also be served frozen. Many people prefer them frozen, and that's almost always how I serve them. They defrost pretty quickly, so I always store these in the freezer.

The Best Blondies

PREP TIME **20 MINUTES** | COOK TIME **45 MINUTES** | SERVES **24 BARS**

I've tried plenty of different blondie recipes over years, but none that were just right. I searched for the texture of a good brownie with that classic butterscotch flavour a good blondie should have. These are the best I've ever made.

One secret to this recipe is to mix the butter, brown sugar, egg, and vanilla mixture for several minutes, to dissolve the brown sugar as much as possible. This will help greatly in achieving a chewier texture to these best caramel-y blondies.

1¾ cups flour

½ tsp baking powder

½ tsp salt

1 cup butter

1¾ cups dark brown sugar, firmly packed

3 eggs, large or extra-large

1 tbsp pure vanilla extract

1. Preheat the oven to 325°F. Lightly grease a 9x9-inch baking pan and line with parchment paper.

2. Sift together the flour, baking powder, and salt. Set aside.

3. Melt the butter in the microwave for a few seconds at a time until just melted. The butter should only be lukewarm, not hot. If it gets overheated, let it cool down before continuing.

4. Put the melted butter in the bowl of an electric mixer along with the brown sugar, eggs, and vanilla.

5. Mix on the lowest setting for about 10 minutes. You can also stir the mixture with a wooden spoon for about the same amount of time, or a little longer. The purpose here is to dissolve the brown sugar into the butter and egg mixture as much as possible, to achieve a chewy texture.

6. Fold in the dry ingredients by hand, mixing only enough so that the flour is fully incorporated. When the last streaks of flour disappear, stop. You do not want to over-mix the batter.

7. Spread batter evenly into the prepared pan.

8. Bake for 40-45 minutes.

9. Cool thoroughly in the pan before cutting into squares or bars.

Chocolate Nanaimo Bars

PREP TIME **25 MINUTES** | COOK TIME **30 MINUTES** | SERVES **36 BARS**

FOR THE BASE LAYER

¾ cup butter

⅓ cup sugar

8 tbsp cocoa

2 eggs, beaten

2¼ cups chocolate cookie crumbs (Oreo crumbs work well)

¾ cup unsweetened coconut, fine or medium cut

½ cup chopped walnuts or pecans, toasted

FOR THE FILLING

3 cups icing sugar

⅔ cup butter, at room temperature

3 tbsp cocoa

¾ cup chocolate chips, melted

1 tsp vanilla paste or extract

4 tbsp milk or whipping cream (approximately)

FOR THE TOP LAYER

1 cup chocolate chips

2 tbsp butter

tip > Not a coconut fan? You can just substitute additional nuts for the coconut if you prefer.

A triple-chocolate version of the classic Canadian no-bake treat. I have quite the love affair with Nanaimo bars, having made several versions with different flavours.

The filling for this recipe is a silky-smooth frosting made with melted chocolate chips for a melt-in-your-mouth dream. The result is an intensely chocolate bar, one of the best I've had.

TO MAKE THE BASE LAYER

1. Melt together the butter, sugar, and cocoa over low heat.

2. Add the eggs and continue to cook, stirring constantly to fully cook the egg to a soft scrambled texture.

3. Add the chocolate cookie crumbs, coconut, and walnuts.

4. Mix together until well combined, then press into the bottom of a 9x9-inch baking pan lined with parchment paper.

TO MAKE THE FILLING

1. With an electric mixer, beat together the icing sugar, butter, and cocoa until it just starts to come together.

2. Add the melted chocolate chips and vanilla and beat well, adding just enough milk, 1 or 2 tablespoons at a time, until smooth. This filling should be very stiff but spreadable—much thicker than frosting for a cake, for example. If you think it's too thick, you may add a few drops of milk at a time to bring it to the right consistency.

3. Spread filling evenly over the bottom layer.

4. Chill in the fridge for a couple of hours before adding the chocolate topping.

TO MAKE THE CHOCOLATE TOPPING

1. Heat the chocolate chips and butter over low heat, just until the chocolate is melted. Do not overheat.

2. Spread quickly over the chilled frosted layer.

3. Return to the fridge until the chocolate sets.

4. Cut into squares or bars.

note > As you can see from the photograph, I prefer my Nanaimo bars on the thicker side in terms of height. If you prefer, though, you can prepare this recipe in a 9x13-inch pan rather than a 9x9-inch pan as the recipe states. The only adjustment to make is in the top layer. You will need more chocolate to cover the larger pan properly. Therefore, when using a 9x13-inch pan, use 1½ cups chocolate chips and 3 tbsp butter. This will give you a more standard thickness in your Nanaimo bars. The recipe yield should be about 50 per cent more and have approximately a third fewer calories per bar as well. These freeze very well.

Anzac Cookies

PREP TIME **15 MINUTES** | COOK TIME **12 MINUTES** | SERVES **30 COOKIES**

Anzac cookies are also known as Anzac biscuits in Australia and New Zealand, dating back to about the time of World War I. One origin story is that they were sturdy, wholesome cookies that could withstand the journey when sent to soldiers in action.

They are commonly prepared for Anzac Day, celebrated in New Zealand and Australia on April 25, to commemorate those who served and died in the war. Fascinated by the history of these cookies, I decided to make my own version. They are a perfect cuppa tea cookie.

---

1 cup dried coconut, fine cut

1 cup flour

1 cup rolled oats

½ cup butter

2 tbsp honey

1 cup brown sugar, lightly packed

1 tsp vanilla extract

2 tbsp boiling water

1 tsp baking soda

¾ cup pecans or walnuts, chopped (optional)

1. Preheat the oven to 350°F and line baking sheets with parchment paper.

2. Mix together the coconut, flour, and rolled oats. Set aside.

3. Heat the butter and honey over low heat just until the butter is melted. Do not overheat.

4. Mix in the brown sugar and vanilla extract.

5. Dissolve the baking soda in the boiling water and mix it into the wet mixture.

6. Fold in the dry ingredients until a soft dough forms. If using nuts, fold them in at the same time.

7. Form rounded teaspoons of dough into balls and place on the prepared cookie sheets about 2½ inches apart. Press them down slightly.

8. Bake for 12-15 minutes. The shorter time will make chewier cookies. The longer time will produce crispier cookies.

note > Baking times vary with different baking pans and ovens. You may need to add 1 or 2 minutes to the baking time for crispier cookies. I always suggest baking only a few to start, to experiment with getting the timing right for your particular oven.

9. Cool on a wire rack.

tip > Store these cookies in an airtight container. They freeze very well, too.

Brown Sugar Fudge

PREP TIME **10 MINUTES** | COOK TIME **10 MINUTES + 3 HOURS TO SET** | SERVES **64 SQUARES**

This recipe was inspired by a reader who evoked a childhood memory of mine. As an early baker, I had clipped this recipe, which was printed on a can of Carnation Milk in the early 1970s. I kept many of these labels and handwritten recipes in a small yellow plastic recipe box. I wonder whatever happened to that little box? No doubt it would offer up other little treasures like this one.

Temperature is key with this brown sugar fudge. I highly recommend a digital food thermometer in order to achieve a smooth and creamy caramel result.

½ cup butter (see notes)

2 cups brown sugar, firmly packed

1 cup evaporated milk

1 cup white sugar

1 teaspoon vanilla extract

1 cup pecans or walnuts, toasted and roughly chopped with a chef's knife (optional)

notes > I use salted butter but do not add any additional salt to the recipe. If using unsalted butter, you may add a pinch or two of salt, if you like.

Do not confuse evaporated milk for sweetened condensed milk. This recipe uses undiluted evaporated milk, measured straight from the can.

1. Lightly grease an 8x8-inch pan and line it with parchment paper. (The size is important; see note on page 173.)

2. In a medium-sized saucepan, melt the butter slowly over medium-low heat.

3. Add the brown sugar, evaporated milk, and white sugar. Increase heat to medium.

4. Bring to a gentle, constant boil.

5. Cook until the mixture reaches between 236 and 238°F. Stir only very occasionally, just a couple of times. Over-stirring can cause crystallization of the sugar, and your fudge will seize.

6. As soon as the mixture hits the correct temperature, remove the pan from the heat.

7. Quickly but gently stir in the vanilla extract.

8. Allow this mixture to sit until lukewarm. Do NOT try to speed this process up by placing it in the fridge or freezer.

9. When cooled to lukewarm, beat the fudge mixture with a wooden spoon until it loses its glossy appearance and begins to thicken more.

10. If adding nuts, stir them in at this point.

note > If adding nuts, you should toast them beforehand for best flavour and crunchy texture. Simply place them in a single layer on a cookie sheet and bake at 350°F for 8-10 minutes, turning them over at about the halfway point.

11. Pour evenly into the prepared pan.

12. Leave for several hours at room temperature to set until firm.

13. Lift the fudge out of the pan using the parchment paper, and transfer it to a cutting board.

14. Cut into 64 one-inch squares, or larger if you prefer.

notes > Store in an airtight container. I do like to refrigerate mine once it is cooled completely and cut.

If freezing fudge, cut the batch into 4 equal squares, and wrap each one tightly with plastic wrap before placing in an airtight container to freeze. This will allow you to take out one or two of the larger pieces and then cut them into portions as needed.

I used light brown sugar in this version and the fudge had plenty of caramel flavour when finished.

to use a larger pan >

This recipe is meant for an 8x8-inch pan. Using a larger pan will produce pieces of fudge that are too thin. The measurements for this recipe using a 9x9-inch pan are:

2½ cups **brown sugar**, firmly packed

1¼ cup **evaporated milk**

1¼ cups **white sugar**

½ cup + 2 tbsp **butter**

1¼ tsp **vanilla extract**

The instructions do not change.

Mars Bars Squares

PREP TIME **10 MINUTES** | COOK TIME **10 MINUTES + 3 HOURS TO SET** | SERVES **64 SQUARES**

This is a very quick and simple recipe for when you need a candy bar fix. It's really an adaptation of Rice Krispie treats using melted Mars bars. I've often seen them on bakery shelves here in Newfoundland but only recently made them myself.

Was I ever missing out! The result is a crispy, chewy, chocolate caramel treat. These squares are perfect to freeze for the holiday season, or for a sweet fix whenever you may need one!

---

6 Mars bars (52 g size)

⅔ cup butter

4 cups crispy rice cereal

FOR THE TOP LAYER

⅓ cup butter

1¼ cups chocolate chips

1. Lightly grease a 9x9-inch baking pan and line it with parchment paper.

2. Chop the Mars bars into small pieces.

3. In a medium-sized saucepan over low heat, melt the ⅔ cup butter.

4. Add the Mars bars and stir constantly until the candy bar pieces are fully melted and smoothly incorporated into the butter.

5. Remove from heat and quickly stir in the crispy rice cereal.

6. Press evenly into the bottom of the prepared pan and chill for about 1 hour before adding the chocolate topping.

TO MAKE THE BASE LAYER

1. Melt the ⅓ cup of butter in a double boiler over low heat.

2. Add the chocolate chips (see note) and stir constantly until the chocolate is completely melted.

notes > I have used milk chocolate chips for the topping on these bars, because I thought it was more in keeping with the chocolate on a Mars candy bar. However, if you want to use semisweet or dark chocolate chips, that's perfectly fine too.

These bars can be stored in the freezer in an airtight container for up to 3 months.

to construct the bars >

1. Pour topping evenly over the cookie base and let set until firm, before cutting into squares or bars.

White Chocolate Nanaimo Bars

PREP TIME **25 MINUTES** | COOK TIME **30 MINUTES + 2 HOURS TO COOL** | SERVES **36 BARS**

FOR THE BOTTOM LAYER

¾   cup butter

⅓   cup sugar

8   tbsp cocoa

2   eggs, beaten

2¼ cups chocolate cookie crumbs (Oreo crumbs work well)

¾   cup unsweetened coconut, fine or medium cut

½   cup chopped walnuts or pecans, toasted

FOR THE FILLING

3   cups icing sugar

⅔   cup butter, at room temperature

3   tbsp cocoa

¾   cup white chocolate chips, melted

1   tsp vanilla paste or extract

4   tbsp milk or whipping cream (approximately)

FOR THE TOP LAYER

1   cup white chocolate chips

2   tbsp butter

Okay, so maybe I am a bit obsessed with Nanaimo bars. Every year, I try to come up with new cookie ideas and twists on old favourites. This was my eighth Nanaimo bar variation!

This white chocolate version proved to be a fast favourite of the folks who follow *RockRecipes.com*. These bars are quite rich and are certain to satisfy even the most demanding sweet tooth.

TO MAKE THE BASE LAYER

1.   Melt together the butter and sugar over low heat.

2.   Add the eggs and continue to cook, stirring constantly to fully cook the egg to a soft scrambled texture.

3.   Add the graham cracker crumbs, coconut, and almonds, and mix together until well combined.

4.   Press mixture into the bottom of a 9x9-inch baking pan lined with parchment paper.

TO MAKE THE FILLING

1.   With an electric mixer, beat together the icing sugar and butter until it just starts to come together.

2.   Add the melted chips and vanilla extract and beat well, adding just enough milk, 1 or 2 tablespoons at a time, until smooth. This filling should be very stiff but spreadable—much thicker than frosting for a cake, for example. If you think it's too thick, you may add a few drops of milk at a time to bring it to the right consistency.

3.   Spread the mixture evenly over the bottom layer.

4.   Chill in the fridge for a couple of hours before adding the white chocolate topping.

TO MAKE THE TOPPING

1. Melt together the white chocolate chips and whipping cream over low heat, just until the chocolate is melted. Do not overheat it. A double boiler is best for this purpose.

2. Allow the melted mixture to cool to room temperature.

3. Use a hand mixer to beat the cooled white chocolate mixture, until it stiffens enough to spread like a soft frosting.

4. Spread evenly over the chilled middle layer and return to the fridge until the chocolate sets.

5. Cut into squares or bars.

note > As you can see from the photograph, I prefer my Nanaimo bars on the thicker side, in terms of height. If you prefer, you can prepare this recipe in a 9x13-inch pan rather than a 9x9-inch pan as the recipe states. The only adjustment to make is in the top layer. You will need more chocolate to cover the larger pan properly, so increase the white chocolate chips to 1½ cups and the whipping cream to 6 tbsp. These freeze very well.

If you've followed my blog or read my previous cookbooks, you'll know I have a thing for cakes. There are several hundred cake recipes on *RockRecipes.com* to date and still growing, rivalling only our extensive collection of cookie recipes.

Homemade cakes from scratch were some of the first things I baked as a kid and the reason for early compliments that encouraged more baking. Those early successes slowly but surely led me to my present-day path.

Over the years, I have heard from thousands of folks who made one of my cakes for special occasions in their lives. I feel like I have been a small part of countless birthdays, anniversaries, bridal and baby showers, even weddings.

It really makes me happy to have made a small contribution to all of those celebrations, and I hope, soon, to one of yours too.

cakes

Jamaican Rum Cake

PREP TIME 20 MINUTES | **COOK TIME 1 HOUR** | **SERVES 16**

This recipe is the successful result of my many attempts to recreate the absolutely perfect rum cake I sampled years ago in Jamaica. It's a dense yet moist cake infused with the secret weapon of a rum and butter syrup that just takes the deliciousness to a whole other level.

Proof of its deliciousness lies in the fact that, over a few days, Spouse and I ate the first one of these I ever baked, all by ourselves! We usually share treats like this with friends and neighbours. Not this one. We hoarded every delicious crumb for ourselves. Utterly irresistible!

FOR THE CAKE

2¼	cups **flour**
1¼	cups **sugar**
½	cup **butter**, soft
¼	cup **canola oil** (or other vegetable oil)
¼	cup **cornstarch**
3	tsp **baking powder**
½	tsp **salt**
½	cup **evaporated milk** (undiluted, straight from the can)
4	**eggs**
⅓	cup **rum** (I use amber rum)
1	tbsp **pure vanilla extract**

FOR THE RUM AND BUTTER SYRUP

½	cup **sugar**
¼	cup **butter**
¼	cup **water**
½-¾	cup **rum** (I use amber rum)
½	tsp **vanilla extract**

TO MAKE THE CAKE

1. Preheat oven to 325°F. Grease and flour a Bundt pan or funnel pan.

2. To the bowl of an electric mixer, add the flour, sugar, butter, oil, cornstarch, baking powder, and salt.

3. Mix on low speed for just a couple of minutes until the butter and oil are well incorporated and the mixture is crumbly and sandy looking.

4. Mix in the milk and then mix in the eggs, one at a time. Scrape the sides and bottom of the bowl well after each egg is added.

5. Finally, mix in the rum and vanilla extract until the batter is smooth.

6. Pour the batter into the prepared pan and bake for 55-65 minutes or until a wooden toothpick inserted into the centre comes out clean.

7. Completely cool the cake on a wire rack.

notes > This cake remains moist for days. The cake was just as good on day four as it was on day one. It didn't see a day five.

This cake needs no frosting or glaze. It is perfect as it is. I think a frosting might make it a little too sweet.

TO MAKE THE RUM AND BUTTER SYRUP

1. Place the sugar, butter, and water in your smallest saucepan. Bring to a slow boil and simmer for 7 or 8 minutes.

2. Remove from the heat and allow to cool completely before adding in the rum and vanilla extract. The amount of rum you add to the syrup is completely up to you. I like it with the full ¾ cup, but you can use less if you want a less rummy cake.

to add the syrup to the cake >

1. Place the cooled cake back in the Bundt pan. This traps in any syrup that drips over the edges and then absorbs it into the cake.
2. With a long skewer, poke holes all over the top of the cake, straight through to the bottom of the pan.
3. Slowly spoon all of the rum and butter syrup evenly over the surface of the cake.
4. Cover the pan with plastic wrap and leave for several hours or overnight.
5. Store in an airtight plastic cake container at room temperature.

Spanish Bar Cake

PREP TIME **20 MINUTES** | COOK TIME **35 MINUTES** | SERVES **12-16**

This cake came at the request of a reader who remembered it fondly from childhood. I have since heard from countless people who shared that memory.

Turns out this cake was made by Jane Parker Bakery and sold through the A&P supermarket chain in the US and Canada. From what I can ascertain, there were regional differences in the recipe, but this one stays true to the moist, delicious, old-fashioned raisin spice cake that so many loved and still remember so well.

note > This recipe also makes about a dozen cupcakes, if you prefer.

FOR THE CAKE

- 2 cups **water**
- 1 cup **raisins**
- ½ cup **vegetable shortening,** or butter
- 2 cups **all-purpose flour**
- 1 cup **granulated sugar**
- 1 tsp **baking soda**
- ½ tsp **ground allspice**
- ½ tsp **ground cinnamon**
- ½ tsp **ground cloves**
- ½ tsp **ground nutmeg**
- ½ tsp **salt**
- 1 large **egg**, beaten
- ½ cup **walnuts** or **pecans**, chopped (optional)

FOR THE FROSTING

- 2¼ cups **icing sugar**
- ¼ cup **butter**, at room temperature
- ½ tsp **pure vanilla**
- 1-2 tablespoons **milk**, more if needed

TO MAKE THE CAKE

1. Preheat the oven to 325°F. Grease a 9x13-inch baking pan and line it with parchment paper.

2. Put the water and raisins in a saucepan. Bring to a gentle boil and simmer for 10 minutes.

3. Add the shortening to the boiled mixture. Allow the mixture to cool to room temperature.

4. Sift together the flour, sugar, soda, allspice, cinnamon, cloves, nutmeg, and salt.

5. Add the sifted ingredients to the cooled raisin mixture, along with the beaten egg and the nuts, if you are using them.

6. Fold gently until the flour is just incorporated into the batter. Do not over-mix.

7. Pour the batter evenly into the prepared pan and bake for 30-35 minutes or until a wooden toothpick inserted into the centre comes out clean.

8. Cool completely and ice with frosting, if you like.

TO MAKE THE FROSTING

1. Beat together the icing sugar, butter, vanilla, and 1 tbsp of milk until smooth. If necessary, add more milk until the frosting is a good spreadable consistency.

2. Cut the cake in half, frost the first layer, then top with the second layer and frost again. To get the characteristic lines on top, run the back of a fork over the top frosting in straight lines.

German Chocolate Cake

PREP TIME 40 MINUTES | COOK TIME 35 MINUTES | SERVES 16-24

FOR THE CAKE

2 cups all-purpose flour

2 cups sugar

1 cup brewed black coffee (or prepare a single cup of instant coffee)

1 cup soured milk (just add a tablespoon of vinegar or lemon juice to the milk)

¾ cup cocoa

½ cup vegetable oil

2 eggs

2 tsp baking powder

1 tsp baking soda

1 tsp vanilla extract

½ tsp salt

FOR THE CARAMEL COCONUT PECAN FILLING

2 cups dried coconut, toasted

1½ cups pecans, toasted and lightly chopped (can substitute walnuts)

1 cup brown sugar

1 cup evaporated milk (undiluted, straight from the can)

½ cup butter, melted

3 egg yolks

1 tbsp vanilla extract

FOR THE CHOCOLATE BUTTERCREAM FROSTING (OPTIONAL)

1 cup chocolate chips

4 cups icing sugar (powdered sugar)

1 cup butter

4 tbsp cocoa

3 tbsp milk (approximately)

2 tsp vanilla extract

German Chocolate cake is always a big hit at our house. Often, we just use the caramel coconut pecan frosting in the middle and on top. Here I've added the option of frosting the sides with chocolate buttercream if you like. That makes for a very nice celebration cake.

As always, I try to improve on any standard recipe and this one gets a flavourful twist by toasting the coconut and pecans before adding them to the caramel filling. The resulting flavour boost makes it so much more delicious!

TO MAKE THE CAKE

1. Grease and flour two 9-inch round pans (or one 9x13-inch pan, if you want to make a bar cake).

2. Combine all ingredients in a mixing bowl and beat with an electric mixer for 2 minutes.

3. Pour into cake pan(s) and bake at 350°F for 30-35 minutes or until a toothpick inserted in the centre comes out clean. Cool in pan(s) for 5 minutes before turning out onto a wire rack to cool completely.

TO MAKE THE CARAMEL COCONUT PECAN FILLING

1. First, toast the coconut and pecans so they can cool before using them. I toast pecans at 350°F on an aluminum baking sheet for about 8 minutes, turning them once during the toasting time.

2. I toast the coconut the same way but toss it about every 3 minutes, so that it toasts evenly. Just keep doing that until the toasted coconut reaches a nice brown colour.

3. Put the brown sugar, evaporated milk, melted butter, egg yolks, and vanilla extract in a medium-sized saucepan and cook over medium-low heat, stirring constantly until the mixture begins to boil and thicken. I cook it for about 2-3 minutes after it starts boiling well. It is very important to stir this constantly or it will stick to the bottom and burn. I use a silicone spatula to stir and constantly scrape the entire surface of the bottom of the pot to make sure it does not stick in any one place.

4. Once thickened and bubbling, add the toasted coconut and pecans.

5. Cool the filling to room temperature, stirring occasionally.

TO MAKE THE CHOCOLATE BUTTERCREAM FROSTING

1. Melt the chocolate chips in a double boiler and let cool to almost room temperature.

2. Mix the icing sugar, butter, and cocoa together until the butter is well broken up into small pieces and distributed throughout the sugar. It may still look powdery at this point.

3. Add the melted chocolate chips, 3 tbsp milk, and vanilla extract.

4. Beat together well until smooth, fluffy, and creamy. You can add more milk if you want a softer frosting or a little more icing sugar if you want a stiffer frosting.

to construct the cake >

1. If you made a 9x13-inch cake, slice it in half lengthwise.

2. Spread the caramel coconut pecan filling over the tops of the two round cakes or the two halves of the rectangular cake, then stack the two sections on top of each other.

3. Frost the sides of the cake with the chocolate butter-cream icing if adding that option.

Orange Bundt Cake
with Cointreau Strawberries

PREP TIME **15 MINUTES** | COOK TIME **45 MINUTES** | SERVES **16**

FOR THE CAKE

2 cups sugar

¾ cup butter

2 tsp vanilla extract

zest of 1 large or 2 small oranges, finely minced

3 eggs

1 cup + 1 tbsp all-purpose flour

1 cup + 1 tbsp cake flour

2 tsp baking powder

¾ cup undiluted evaporated milk

FOR THE MARINATED COINTREAU STRAWBERRIES

1½ pints fresh strawberries, washed and sliced

6 tbsp sugar

2 oz Cointreau liqueur (optional)

FOR THE VANILLA WHIPPED CREAM

1 cup whipping cream

2 rounded tbsp icing sugar

1 tsp vanilla extract

At our house we make several desserts that combine orange and strawberry flavours. The orange-flavoured Cointreau liqueur in this one adds a very nice touch to the strawberries, but it is of course optional.

This versatile cake can be as simple as a delicious teatime treat all on its own, or dressed up with those gorgeous Cointreau-macerated strawberries for a celebration dinner or dinner party.

This intensely orange-citrus-flavoured cake will quickly become one of your go-to recipes as well.

TO MAKE THE MARINATED COINTREAU STRAWBERRIES

1. Toss the sliced strawberries, sugar, and Cointreau together well, in a glass bowl. Cover the bowl with plastic wrap and let stand for about 2 hours, stirring occasionally. The sugar will cause the strawberries to begin to release their juice, combining to form a strawberry syrup.

TO MAKE THE CAKE

1. Preheat oven to 325°F and grease and flour a Bundt pan.

2. Cream the sugar, butter, vanilla, and orange zest well.

3. Add the eggs, one at a time, beating well after each addition.

4. In a separate bowl, sift together the all-purpose flour, cake flour, and baking powder.

5. Fold the dry ingredients into the creamed mixture, alternately with the milk. Begin and end with the dry ingredients. I normally add the dry ingredients in 3 portions and the milk in 2 portions.

6. Pour batter into the pan and bake for 40-45 minutes or until a toothpick inserted in the centre comes out clean. Baking times vary depending upon the size of your Bundt pan, so the toothpick test is the best method to ensure that the cake is completely baked.

7. Cool completely on a wire rack before topping with vanilla whipped cream and Cointreau strawberries.

TO MAKE THE VANILLA WHIPPED CREAM

1. Simply whip the whipping cream, icing sugar, and vanilla extract together until soft peaks form.

Coconut Velvet Cake

PREP TIME **25** MINUTES | COOK TIME **35** MINUTES | SERVES **16**

FOR THE CAKE

- 1½ cups **cake flour**, sifted
- 1½ cups **sugar**
- 1¼ cup **all-purpose flour**, sifted
- 1½ tsp **baking powder**
- ½ tsp **baking soda**
- 1 tsp **salt**
- ⅓ cup **vegetable oil**
- ⅓ cup **vegetable shortening** at room temperature
- 2 tsp **pure coconut extract**
- 1 tsp **vanilla extract**
- 3 **eggs**, large
- 1½ cups **coconut milk**
- ¼ cup **milk**
- ¼-⅓ cup **dried coconut** to add to the batter (optional)

FOR THE FROSTING

- 1¼ cups **sugar**
- ½ cup **corn syrup**
- ¼ cup **water**
- 4 **egg whites**
- ¼ tsp **cream of tarter**
- 1½ tsp **pure coconut extract**
- 1 tsp **vanilla extract**
- 1 cup **dried coconut** (approximately), sweetened or unsweetened (see note on page 191 if you want to use toasted coconut)

Coconut lovers rejoice! Your ultimate cake is within your grasp.

Our velvet cake recipes are always incredibly popular. Our Red Velvet, Spice Velvet, and Lemon Velvet versions have also appeared in two of my previous cookbooks.

This new coconut version is a beautifully moist and tender crumbed cake. It's flavoured with coconut milk and coconut extract, then covered in a coconut marshmallow frosting and a generous garnish of dried coconut. It's a coconut lover's dream.

TO MAKE THE CAKE

1. Preheat oven to 325°F. Grease and flour two 9-inch round cake pans and line the bottom of each with a circle of parchment paper.

2. Sift together both flours, sugar, baking powder, baking soda, and salt. Set aside.

3. In the bowl of an electric mixer, beat together the vegetable oil, shortening, coconut extract, and vanilla. Beat well at high speed with whisk attachment until light and fluffy.

4. Beat the eggs in, one at a time.

5. Mix together the coconut milk and milk.

6. Fold the dry ingredients into the egg and oil mixture alternately with the coconut milk mixture. I always add dry ingredients in 3 portions and liquid ingredients in 2 portions. It is very important to begin and end the additions with the dry ingredients. Do not over-mix the batter. As soon as it has no lumps in the batter, pour into the two prepared pans.

7. Bake for 30-35 minutes or until a wooden toothpick inserted in the centre comes out clean. Allow the cake to cool in the pans for 10 minutes before turning out onto wire racks to cool completely.

TO MAKE THE COCONUT MARSHMALLOW FROSTING

1. In a small saucepan, combine sugar, corn syrup, and water. Bring to a boil over medium heat and continue to cook until the mixture reaches 240°F on a candy thermometer or when a teaspoonful of the mixture dropped into ice water forms a soft ball that holds its shape when cool.

2. In a large bowl, whip the egg whites, cream of tartar, and vanilla and coconut extracts to soft peaks.

3. With the mixer on medium-high speed, slowly begin to pour the sugar syrup down the side of the egg white bowl in a thin continuous stream.

Toasted coconut is good if you use unsweetened dried coconut; the sweetened coconut tends to burn more easily when toasted.

to toast unsweetened coconut >
Preheat the oven to 350°F and spread the coconut on a baking sheet. Bake for about 5-7 minutes or until the coconut begins to turn golden brown. I like to toss the coconut once or twice during the baking time to ensure even browning.

4. Continue to whip the frosting until it forms stiff peaks.

5. Frost your cake immediately while the frosting is still slightly warm as it is easier to spread smoothly than if allowed to cool completely.

6. Immediately cover the top and sides of the cake with dried coconut.

Jam Jam Cake

PREP TIME **20** MINUTES | COOK TIME **40** MINUTES | SERVES **16**

For those of you who have never heard of them, Jam Jams are an iconic Newfoundland cookie treat from Purity Factories, which has been in operation since 1924. They are soft cake-y molasses cookies, sandwiched together with partridgeberry-apple jam and have been loved by Newfoundlanders for generations.

After a recent disappointment with a local restaurant's take on a Jam Jam Cake, I set out to develop my own recipe. With just the right level of molasses flavour in the cake and a delicious jam filling, I call this Newfoundland's answer to the UK's Victoria Sandwich Cake. It makes a terrific Sunday dinner dessert, especially when entertaining come-from-aways, a.k.a. mainlanders.

1½ cups **cake flour**, sifted

1¼ cups **all-purpose flour**, sifted

1½ tsp **baking powder**

½ tsp **baking soda**

½ tsp **salt**

½ cup **butter**, at room temperature

½ cup **light brown sugar**

½ cup **vegetable oil**

1 tsp **vanilla extract**

3 **eggs**, large

¾ cup **evaporated milk**, undiluted

¾ cup **fancy molasses** (not cooking molasses)

1 cup **partridgeberry apple jam**, or any red berry jam you like

icing sugar (powdered sugar) to garnish (optional)

1. Preheat oven to 325°F. Grease and flour two 8-inch round cake pans and line the bottom of each with a circle of parchment paper.

2. Sift together both flours, baking powder, baking soda, and salt. Set aside.

3. In the bowl of an electric mixer, beat together butter, brown sugar, vegetable oil, and vanilla. Beat well at high speed with whisk attachment until light and fluffy.

4. Beat the eggs in, one at a time.

5. Mix together the milk and molasses until well blended.

6. Fold the dry ingredients into the butter mixture alternately with the molasses/milk combination. I always add dry ingredients in 3 portions and liquid ingredients in 2 portions. It is very important to begin and end the additions with the dry ingredients.

7. Do not over-mix the batter. As soon as it has no lumps, pour the batter into the pans and bake for 35-40 minutes or until a wooden toothpick inserted in the centre comes out clean.

8. Allow the cake to cool in the pans for 10 minutes before turning out onto wire racks to cool completely.

9. Spread the jam between the layers and sprinkle a little icing sugar on to garnish, if you like.

2 lbs fresh strawberries, washed

FOR THE CAKE

2 cups all-purpose flour

2 cups sugar

1 cup **black brewed coffee**, or just prepare instant coffee

1 cup **soured milk** (to sour, add 1 tbsp lemon juice or vinegar)

¾ cup **cocoa**

½ cup **vegetable oil**

2 **eggs**

2 tsp **baking powder**

1 tsp **baking soda**

1 tsp **vanilla extract**

½ tsp **salt**

FOR THE FILLING

2 cups **dark chocolate chips** (50% cocoa or higher)

2 cups **whipping cream** (½ cup and 1½ cups)

2 rounded tbsp **icing sugar**

FOR THE GLAZE

3 tbsp **butter**

1½ tbsp **corn syrup**

¾ cup **chocolate chips**

Chocolate Whipped Cream Cake *with* Strawberries and Chocolate Ganache Glaze

PREP TIME **30 MINUTES** | COOK TIME **35 MINUTES** | SERVES **16**

As I sit here, rewriting this recipe from a few years back, I am reminded that it's just a week and a half to Mother's Day. Coincidentally, that's the same occasion for which I created this recipe back in 2017.

Incredibly, I have posted over three hundred cake recipes to *RockRecipes.com* in the last thirteen years. Plenty of them are celebration cakes like this one.

Many of them are also easy to prepare but leave a stunning impression. That's my favourite kind of cake. Why not enjoy this one on your next occasion, even if it's just dinner with friends?

TO MAKE THE CAKE

1. Preheat oven to 350°F. Grease and flour two 8- or 9-inch cake pans.

2. Combine all ingredients in a mixing bowl and beat with electric mixer for 2 minutes.

3. Pour batter evenly into the two cake pans and bake for 30-35 minutes or until toothpick inserted in the centre comes out clean.

4. Cool in pans for 5 minutes before turning out onto a wire rack to cool completely.

TO MAKE THE FILLING

1. In a small saucepan over low heat, scald ½ cup of the whipping cream. Do not let it boil.

2. Add the chocolate chips and stir just until they melt. You do not want to overheat the chocolate here. Stir off the heat, returning the pan to the heat only for 20 seconds at time until the chocolate is completely smooth.

3. Whip the remaining 1½ cups whipping cream and the icing sugar together to form peaks.

4. Using a whisk, fold the chocolate gently through the whipped cream in about 3 equal portions until thoroughly incorporated.

TO MAKE THE GHOCOLATE GANACHE GLAZE

1. Melt the butter in a small saucepan and add the corn syrup. When this mixture just begins to barely simmer, remove from the heat and stir in the chocolate chips.

2. Stir until the chocolate is completely melted and the glaze is smooth and glossy.

3. If need be, return the pan to the heat for a minute to completely melt the chocolate.

to construct the cake >

1. Clean and hull enough strawberries to cover the top of one of the cakes, standing with the point up. Choose strawberries about the same size or cut the bases down to equalize their height.

2. Place the bottom layer of cake on a cake plate and spread on a thin layer of the chocolate whipped cream filling.

3. Next, add the strawberries, with the tips pointing up. Place them closely together to cover the entire bottom layer of cake.

4. Next, add the remaining whipped chocolate cream to cover the top and sides of the strawberries completely. Push it between the strawberries to fill any gaps.

5. Refrigerate the cake for a couple of hours to let the filling set completely

6. Add the top layer of cake and pour the ganache on, using a decorating spatula or the back of a tablespoon to spread it evenly, and let it drip down over the sides.

7. Garnish with additional fresh strawberries, if you like, before serving.

White Velvet Strawberry Shortcake

PREP TIME **30** MINUTES | COOK TIME **40** MINUTES | SERVES **12** OR MORE

FOR THE CAKE

1½	cups **cake flour**, sifted
1½	cups **sugar**
1¼	cups **all-purpose flour**, sifted
1½	tsp **baking powder**
½	tsp **salt**
½	tsp **baking soda**
⅔	cup **vegetable oil**
⅓	cup **vegetable shortening**, at room temperature
3	tbsp **vanilla extract** (if you want a pure white cake, use a clear vanilla extract)
3	**eggs**, large (or 4 egg whites for a purely white cake)
1½	cups **buttermilk** (or 1 cup whole milk mixed with 1 tbsp lemon juice)

FOR THE MACERATED STRAWBERRIES

2	quarts **fresh strawberries**, sliced
½-¾	cup **sugar**

FOR THE VANILLA WHIPPED CREAM

1½	cups **whipping cream**
4	tbsp **icing sugar** (powdered sugar)
1½	tsp **pure vanilla extract**

Strawberry shortcake is a real family favourite around here, especially of my daughter Olivia. Her birthday cake is almost always a strawberry shortcake of some kind.

As an everyday dessert treat, I like to bake it as a sheet cake, which makes it even easier to prepare and serve without fuss.

This is an incredibly simple but delicious version of strawberry shortcake on the lightest, most moist homemade white cake you've ever tried.

TO MAKE THE CAKE

1. Preheat oven to 325°F. Grease and flour a 9x13-inch baking pan.

2. Sift together both flours, sugar, baking powder, salt, and baking soda. Set aside.

3. In the bowl of an electric mixer, beat together the vegetable oil, shortening, and vanilla. Beat well at high speed with whisk attachment until light and fluffy.

4. Beat the eggs in, one at a time.

5. Fold in the dry ingredients alternately with the buttermilk. I always add dry ingredients in 3 portions and liquid ingredients in 2 portions. It is very important to begin and end the additions with the dry ingredients. Do not over-mix the batter. As soon as it has no lumps, pour the batter into the prepared 9x13-inch pan.

6. Bake for 40-45 minutes or until a wooden toothpick inserted in the centre comes out clean. Allow the cake to cool in the pan for 10 minutes before turning out onto a wire rack to cool completely.

TO PREPARE THE STRAWBERRIES

1. Wash, hull, and slice the strawberries and place them in a glass bowl.

2. Sprinkle the sugar onto the berries and toss well.

3. Leave to macerate together for about 1 hour, tossing the berries in the sugar/syrup occasionally. This step draws some of the juice from the berries to form a sweet strawberry syrup.

TO MAKE THE VANILLA WHIPPED CREAM

1. Whip the cream, icing sugar, and vanilla extract together to firm peaks.

to construct the cake >

1. When ready to serve, cut the cake into 12 or more portions.

2. Spoon some of the macerated berries onto each cake portion, as well as some of the strawberry syrup, followed by some of the whipped cream.

3. Garnish with a whole fresh berry.

Honey Banana Snack Cake

PREP TIME **10 MINUTES** | COOK TIME **45 MINUTES** | SERVES **12**

Back when I was at school, we often made a similar snack cake from a mix. Spouse and I were recently discussing this, and she reminded me that there was a disposable pan in the box as well. I had completely forgotten that.

This from-scratch honey banana cake inspired by that childhood snack is the quickest and easiest snack cake ever. All ingredients go into one bowl, then it's just mix and bake! It's a quick, super moist, delicious little cake perfect for packed lunches, teatime, and after school snacks.

2	cups **banana puree**
2	cups **all-purpose flour**
1	cup **brown sugar**, lightly packed
⅓	cup **butter**, soft and at room temperature
⅓	cup **honey**
¼	cup **vegetable oil**
2	**eggs**, large or extra-large
2	tsp **vanilla extract**
1½	tsp **baking powder**
½	tsp **baking soda**

1. Preheat oven to 350°F. Lightly grease a 9x9-inch baking pan and line with parchment paper.

2. Mash the bananas. I like to do this in my stand mixer as the first ingredient to add to the bowl. Just mix the ripe bananas at medium speed until they are a smooth puree.

3. Add all of the remaining ingredients and mix for only 1 minute until the batter is smooth.

4. Pour the batter into the prepared pan and bake for 40-45 minutes or until a wooden toothpick inserted in the centre comes out clean.

5. Allow to cool at least 30 minutes before serving.

note > This recipe is made in a 9x9-inch pan, but if you only have enough bananas on hand to make 1 cup of banana puree, you can easily make a smaller snack cake. Just use half this recipe and bake it in a 9x5-inch loaf pan. You can even make the full recipe in 2 loaf pans and freeze one for later.

Joe Louis Cake

PREP TIME **10** MINUTES | COOK TIME **45** MINUTES | SERVES **12**

FOR THE CAKE

- 2 cups **all-purpose flour**
- 2 cups **sugar**
- 1 cup **black coffee**
- 1 cup **soured milk**
- ¾ cup **cocoa**
- ½ cup **vegetable oil**
- 2 **eggs**
- 2 tsp **baking powder**
- 1 tsp **baking soda**
- 1 tsp **vanilla extract**
- ½ tsp **salt**

FOR THE FROSTING

- 1 cup **sugar**
- ⅓ cup **water**
- 3 tbsp **corn syrup**
- 2 **egg whites**
- 1 tsp **vanilla extract**
- ¼ tsp **cream of tartar**

FOR THE GLAZE

- 2 cups **semisweet** or **dark chocolate chips**
- ½ cup **whipping cream**

Based upon the famous Canadian snack cake, this recipe has proven to be one of the most popular dessert cakes ever on *Rock Recipes*. Think of it as three relatively easy recipes that come together into one.

This Joe Louis chocolate, marshmallow-y cake really is a pretty simple dessert with three components: a one-bowl chocolate cake, a marshmallow-like filling, and a rich chocolate ganache glaze. They all come together to make a pretty special celebration cake.

TO MAKE THE CAKE

1. Preheat oven to 350°F. Grease and flour two 9-inch cake pans or one large 10- to 12-inch baking pan.

2. Combine all ingredients in a mixing bowl and beat with an electric mixer for 2 minutes.

3. Pour into pan(s) and bake for 30-35 minutes or until a toothpick inserted in the centre comes out clean. The time will be longer for a larger pan. Cool completely.

TO MAKE THE FROSTING

1. In a small saucepan combine sugar, water, and corn syrup. Bring to a boil over medium heat and continue to cook until the mixture reaches 240°F on a candy thermometer, or when a teaspoonful of the mixture dropped into ice water forms a soft ball that holds its shape when cool.

2. Whip the egg whites, vanilla extract, and cream of tartar to soft peaks in a large bowl. With the mixer on medium-high speed, slowly begin to pour the sugar syrup down the side of the egg white bowl in a thin continuous stream. Continue to whip the frosting until it forms stiff peaks.

3. Fill your cake immediately with the warm frosting as it is easier to spread smoothly than if allowed to cool completely.

TO MAKE THE GLAZE

1. Scald whipping cream almost to boiling and pour over the chocolate chips. Let stand for 3-4 minutes, then stir well until smooth.

2. Split the cake horizontally and cover the bottom half with the frosting. Place the other half on top and spread the chocolate ganache over the entire cake. Allow it to cool before serving.

Irish Coffee Cake

PREP TIME **20** MINUTES | COOK TIME **30** MINUTES | SERVES **16**

We do have a bit of a tradition of celebrating our Irish heritage here in Newfoundland. Over the years, *Rock Recipes* has featured a number of tasty ways to do just that.

Inspired by an Irish Coffee, this is a chocolate stout cake with an easy Baileys Irish Cream frosting. It is the ideal cake for St. Patrick's Day!

FOR THE CAKE

2 cups all-purpose flour

1 pint (2 cups) Guinness stout

2 cups sugar

¾ cup cocoa

½ cup vegetable oil

2 eggs

2 tsp baking powder

1 tsp baking soda

1 tsp vanilla extract

½ tsp salt

FOR THE FROSTING

4 cups icing sugar (powdered sugar)

¾ cup butter

⅓ cup Irish cream liqueur

YOU MIGHT ALSO NEED

2 oz Irish whiskey (optional)

TO MAKE THE CAKE

1. Preheat oven to 350°F. Grease two 9-inch cake pans. I like to use additional cocoa to dust the sides and bottom of the pans instead of flour, and I do usually line the bottom of the cake pans with parchment paper.

2. Combine all ingredients in a mixing bowl and beat with an electric mixer for 2 minutes.

3. Pour batter evenly into the two pans and bake for 30-35 minutes or until a toothpick inserted in the centre comes out clean.

4. Cool in pans for 5 minutes before turning out onto wire racks to cool completely.

5. When cakes are cooled, sprinkle each with one ounce of Irish whiskey, if you choose to use it.

TO MAKE THE FROSTING

1. With an electric mixer, beat together the icing sugar, butter, and Irish cream liqueur until very smooth.

note > This frosting should be easily spreadable. If you think it's too thick, you may add a few drops of Irish cream at a time to bring it to the right consistency. If it is too soft, add a little more icing sugar.

2. Frost the tops of the two cakes, then place one on top of the other.

Apricot Hazelnut Pound Cake

PREP TIME 20 MINUTES | COOK TIME 45 MINUTES
SERVES 32 (1 LARGE CAKE OR 2 SMALLER 8X4-INCH LOAVES)

Longtime readers of my blog will know that I have a particular fondness for anything apricot. Add to that my love of roasted hazelnuts, and I had no doubt in my mind the combination would be a winner.

This favourite, old-fashioned buttery pound cake gets a delicious update with the addition of sweet little apricot chunks paired perfectly with toasted hazelnuts. Another example of old-fashioned baking at its very best.

---

2 cups **sugar**

1½ cups **butter**

3 **eggs**

2 tsp **vanilla extract**

3 cups **flour**

1½ tsp **baking powder**

1 cup **undiluted evaporated milk,** lukewarm

2 cups **dried apricots,** chopped, + ¼ cup flour for tossing

1 cup **hazelnuts,** toasted then roughly chopped

1. Preheat oven to 325°F. Grease and flour a springform pan or a Bundt pan, or line 2 loaf pans with parchment paper.

2. Cream the sugar and butter together well.

3. Add the eggs, one at a time, beating well after each addition until light and fluffy.

4. Beat in the vanilla extract.

5. In a separate bowl, sift together the flour and baking powder.

6. Fold dry ingredients into the creamed mixture alternately with the lukewarm milk, beginning and ending with the dry ingredients. As a general rule, I add the dry ingredients in 3 portions and the milk in 2 portions.

7. Toss the chopped apricots in ¼ cup flour then fold them in, along with the chopped hazelnuts.

8. Pour the batter into your chosen pan(s) and bake for 45-60 minutes, depending upon the size of your pan. Baking times vary greatly on this recipe, so rely on the toothpick test to ensure that it is properly baked. When a wooden toothpick inserted in the centre comes out clean, it's done. Be careful not to go past this stage or the cake will be dry.

9. Let the cake cool in the pan(s) for 10 minutes before turning it out onto a wire rack to cool completely.

I live by the motto that no great meal is complete without a great dessert. It is the finale of any enjoyable meal and the cook's final bow.

It's what people are served last that makes the meal memorable. A mediocre meal can be salvaged with an outstanding dessert, and conversely, a mediocre dessert can put a bit of a damper on an otherwise stellar meal.

Dessert also says to your family, friends, and guests that they were worth going the extra mile for, to make a meal special. It's like adding extra love to any occasion.

desserts

Lemon Mousse Trifle

PREP TIME **50** MINUTES | COOK TIME **30** MINUTES | SERVES **12-16**

FOR THE CAKE

4 oz limoncello liqueur (optional)

candied lemon peel (optional)

FOR THE LEMON CURD

1 cup flour

1 tsp baking powder

6 eggs, separated, at room temperature

¼ tsp cream of tartar

1 cup sugar, separated into 2 half cups

2 tsp vanilla extract

½ tsp lemon flavouring (optional)

FOR THE LEMON CURD

6 egg yolks, lightly beaten

1 cup sugar

½ cup fresh lemon juice

zest of 2 lemons, finely minced

½ cup butter, cut into small pieces

FOR THE LEMON MOUSSE

4 cups whipping cream

4 rounded tbsp icing sugar (powdered sugar)

1 tsp vanilla extract

1 batch lemon curd, previously prepared and chilled

I love desserts with layers of the same flavour, interpreted in different ways. I packed as much lemon punch as I could into this one.

This trifle really is a simple combination of sponge cake, whipped cream, and lemon curd with a little extra citrus punch from limoncello liqueur. The liqueur is purely optional; you may choose not to use it.

It's a simple but delectable dessert fit for any lemon lover, not to mention perfect for serving a crowd.

TO MAKE THE SPONGE CAKE

1. Preheat oven to 325°F. Line the bottoms of two 8-inch round cake pans, but do not grease the sides.

2. Sift together the flour and baking powder and set aside.

3. For the meringue base of the batter, beat egg whites and cream of tartar until foamy.

4. Add ½ cup sugar gradually until egg whites are stiff.

5. In a separate bowl, beat egg yolks and ½ cup sugar until foamy and thickened.

6. Fold beaten egg yolks into the beaten egg whites along with the vanilla and lemon flavouring for only a few turns, before slowly and gradually folding in the flour and baking powder mixture very gently BY HAND, using a rubber spatula until just incorporated into the meringue mixture. I mix in the dry ingredients in 3 equal portions. Do not over-mix, you want the flour to be just incorporated. Over-mixing will deflate the egg whites and result in a tough texture.

7. Bake for 25-30 minutes or until the centre springs back when touched.

8. Cool completely in the pans. This prevents the cake from shrinking as it cools.

9. When completely cooled, run a small sharp knife completely around the outside edge of the pan to release the cake. Do this slowly, being sure to keep the knife at a steady 90-degree angle so you don't damage the sides of the cake. Turn the cakes out onto a wire rack and peel off the parchment paper on the bottom.

10. Cut the cooled sponge cakes into small cubes for the trifle.

TO MAKE THE LEMON CURD

1. In a small saucepan combine the egg yolks, sugar, lemon juice, and zest.

2. Cook slowly over medium-low heat for about 10 minutes, stirring constantly until the mixture thickens enough to coat the back of a wooden spoon.

3. Remove from heat and stir in the butter a few pieces at a time until completely smooth. Cover with plastic wrap and chill completely in the fridge.

tip > If you like lemon curd that's a little less intense in flavour, use the zest of only 1 lemon; about 1 tbsp should be fine.

MAKE THE LEMON MOUSSE

1. Whip the cream, icing sugar, and vanilla extract to firm peaks. Remove about ¼ of the whipped cream and reserve it for the top of the trifle.

2. Using a rubber spatula, fold the chilled lemon curd through the whipped cream until thoroughly blended.

CONTINUED ON PAGE 210 >

to construct the trifle >

1. Place ¼ of the cake cubes in the bottom of the trifle bowl and sprinkle with 1 oz of the limoncello, if you are using it.

2. Spoon on ⅓ of the lemon mousse mixture (or ½ if you plan the extra lemon curd layer at the center; see note).

3. Repeat the layers until you finish with a final layer of cake and sprinkle on the remaining limoncello.

4. Add the reserved whipped cream on top. Garnish with candied lemon peel, if you like. Chill the trifle for several hours or even overnight before serving.

note > The middle layer of lemon curd as pictured is optional in this recipe. If you want to add it, I recommend making 1½ times the lemon curd recipe, or even double if you love lemon curd as much as I do.

Brownie Cheesecake

PREP TIME **40 MINUTES** | COOK TIME **1 HOUR 10 MINUTES** | SERVES **16**

FOR THE CHEESECAKE

1⅓ cups chocolate cookie crumbs

⅓ cup butter, melted

3 tbsp sugar

3 eight-ounce packages of cream cheese (3 cups total)

1 cup sugar

3 eggs

3 tsp vanilla extract

1 cup whipping cream

FOR THE FILLING

½ cup + 1 rounded tbsp flour

3 tbsp cocoa powder

pinch salt

⅓ cup butter

3½ squares unsweetened chocolate (or about ½ cup dark chocolate chips), melted

½ cup + 1 rounded tbsp granulated sugar

3 rounded tbsp light-brown sugar

1 egg, extra-large

1 tsp vanilla extract

FOR THE CHOCOLATE GANACHE

¼ cup whipping cream

½ cup dark chocolate chips

A luscious, creamy vanilla cheesecake sits atop a chocolate cookie crumb crust, topped with mounds of mini brownies and a drizzle of rich chocolate ganache.

Topping the plain vanilla cheesecake with mini brownies preserves their chewy, fudgy texture, as well as the creaminess of a perfectly baked cheesecake. It's an outstanding mix of textures and flavours.

TO MAKE THE CHEESECAKE

1. Preheat oven to 300°F. Line a 9-inch springform pan with parchment paper (or lightly grease the bottom only). Parchment paper is ideal here because it makes it very easy to release the cheesecake from the bottom of the pan.

2. In a small bowl, combine the cookie crumbs, melted butter, and sugar, then press into the bottom of the pan.

3. Cream together the cream cheese and 1 cup sugar until smooth.

4. Add the eggs one at a time, beating well after each addition.

5. Beat in the vanilla extract.

6. Finally, blend in the whipping cream.

7. Pour over the prepared base and bake in a *bain-marie* (see note) for 60-70 minutes. The cheesecake does not have to brown at all in order to be fully baked; when the cake is properly baked, the surface of the cheesecake will lose any shine. It can still be slightly wobbly just at the centre at this point.

8. Remove the cake from the oven and run a sharp knife completely around the edge of the pan. This will allow for the cheesecake to shrink as it cools and hopefully not crack (but who cares if it does? I am never bothered by a crack or two on the surface). Allow the cheesecake to cool thoroughly on a wire rack at room temperature, not in the fridge. Refrigerate after fully cooled.

9. Top with the mini brownies and drizzle with chocolate ganache before serving.

TO MAKE THE FILLING

1. Preheat oven to 325°F. Grease an 8-inch square baking pan and line it with parchment paper.

2. Sift together flour, cocoa, and salt.

3. Melt together butter and unsweetened chocolate over low heat. Do not let this mixture overheat.

4. Remove from heat and cool to lukewarm.

5. Add sugars, egg, and vanilla. Stir very well until sugars are almost dissolved.

6. Gently fold in dry ingredients.

7. Pour batter into pan and bake for about 15-18 minutes or until the surface of the centre of the brownies appears dry and firm. Toothpick test will not work for this recipe, but it will tell you if the middle is still liquid. Do not ove-bake these brownies or they will be dry rather than moist and chewy.

8. Cool completely before cutting into ½-inch squares.

TO MAKE THE CHOCOLATE GANACHE

1. In a double boiler, melt together the whipping cream and chocolate chips

2. Drizzle over the brownies and cheesecake.

to bake cheesecake in a *bain-marie* >

A *bain-marie* is simply a water bath that buffers the direct heat from the sides and bottom of the baking pan to more evenly bake the cheesecake from the sides to the centre. I bake my cheesecakes in a 9-inch springform pan that has the bottom and sides wrapped in multiple layers of wide, heavy-duty aluminum foil, which forms a sort of boat that the cheesecake pan sits in. The roll of aluminum foil I use is about 16 inches wide. I use at least 4 layers of foil to make sure that no water leaks in and ruins the crust of my cheesecake. The aluminum foil-wrapped pan is then placed inside a larger baking pan. I use a 12-inch cake pan. Boiling water is then poured into the larger pan, filling it from ½ to ⅔ of the way to the top.

I find it best to pour the boiling water into the pan after it is placed on the rack in the oven, as you are less likely to splash water onto the cheesecake or inside the aluminum foil. I reuse the aluminum foil for several future cheesecakes, adding a couple of layers to it each time, just to be safe.

Blueberry Gingerbread Cake
with Toffee Sauce

PREP TIME **20 MINUTES** | COOK TIME **1 HOUR 15 MINUTES** | SERVES **16**

This moist and beautifully spiced gingerbread cake is bursting with blueberries and gets served warm with an easy-to-make toffee sauce.

Spouse in particular loves a warm comfort food dessert and is a fanatic for anything gingerbread. The house will smell of Christmas as the heady scent of spices wafts through every corner.

FOR THE CAKE

3½ cups flour

1½ tbsp powdered ginger

1   tbsp ground cinnamon

1½ tsp ground nutmeg

1   tsp baking powder

1   tsp ground allspice

½   tsp baking soda

½   tsp ground cloves

1   cup milk

⅔   cup molasses

1½ cups brown sugar, lightly packed

1   cup butter, salted

3   eggs, large

1   tsp vanilla extract

2½ cups blueberries, fresh or frozen

FOR THE TOFFEE SAUCE

1   cup whipping cream

½   cup butter

½   cup brown sugar, firmly packed

4   tbsp golden syrup or corn syrup

2   tbsp molasses

2   tsp vanilla extract

TO MAKE THE CAKE

1.   Preheat the oven to 350°F. Grease a large Bundt pan or tube pan well, and dust the inside lightly with cinnamon.

2.   Sift together the flour, spices, baking powder, and baking soda. Set aside.

3.   Stir together the milk and molasses until well blended and the molasses is fully mixed into the milk. Set aside.

4.   Cream together the butter and brown sugar until light and fluffy, about 5 minutes.

5.   Add the eggs to the butter mixture, one at a time, beating well after each addition. Beat in the vanilla extract.

6.   Fold in the dry ingredients into the creamed mixture alternately with the molasses and milk mixture. Always begin and end with the dry ingredients. As a general rule I add the dry ingredients in 3 portions and the liquid in 2 portions.

7.   When the last of the dry ingredients is almost fully incorporated, add the blueberries for the final few folds of the batter.

8. Spread the batter evenly into the prepared Bundt pan and bake for about 1 hour and 15 minutes, or until a wooden toothpick inserted into the centre of the cake comes out clean. I generally start checking about 10 minutes before the baking time is up. Using frozen berries will extend the baking time.

note > This cake can also be made in 2 small loaf pans if you prefer.

TO MAKE THE TOFFEE SAUCE

1. Bring all of the ingredients to a slow rolling boil for about 2 minutes before serving over slices of the cake.

> **tip** > You can use flour to dust the pan after it is greased if you prefer, but cinnamon is my trick for keeping those white marks of flour off the edges of the cake. I do the same thing with cocoa when making chocolate cake.

Lemon Pudding Cake

PREP TIME **20 MINUTES** | COOK TIME **40 MINUTES** | SERVES **8-10**

FOR THE LEMON SAUCE

1¼ cups sugar

2 tbsp cornstarch

pinch of salt

3 egg yolks

1½ cups water

juice of 2 large lemons
(Remove the zest from both
lemons before juicing them.
Half the zest will go in the
sauce and half will go in the
cake.)

zest of 1 large lemon,
  very finely minced

4 tbsp butter (not
  margarine)

FOR THE LEMON CAKE

½ cup sugar

⅓ cup butter

1 egg

1 tsp vanilla extract

zest of 1 large lemon, finely
  minced

1½ cups flour

1 tsp baking powder

½ cup milk

An ultimate lemon comfort food dessert that combines a bright, flavourful lemon cake baked on top of a tart, tangy, not too sweet lemon sauce.

I developed this recipe in an attempt to replicate one of my childhood favourite desserts in a delectable homemade version. This is a must-try for any lemon lover.

TO MAKE THE LEMON SAUCE

1. In a small saucepan, combine the sugar, cornstarch, and salt.

2. While still off the heat, whisk in the egg yolks.

3. Add the water, lemon juice, and zest, and place over medium-low heat.

4. Bring this mixture to a boil, stirring constantly. I find that a silicone spatula is best for this because you can continuously scrape the entire bottom of the pan, making sure that the sauce thickens evenly and doesn't stick or burn.

5. Once it is boiling, continue to boil for 1 minute, then take it off the heat and stir in the butter, a tablespoon at a time, until smooth.

6. Pour into an ungreased 8-cup casserole dish or a pan of similar size that is about 4 inches deep.

7. Set aside while you prepare the cake batter.

note > People ask me what I mean by finely minced lemon zest. My method is to use the fine side of a box grater placed on a cutting board to remove all of the zest from the lemon, while avoiding as much of the bitter white part of the peel as possible. I then take a chef's knife and continue to chop the finely grated zest into small bits. Using this method, I rarely ever strain a lemon curd or sauce through a sieve after it is cooked. The zest left in a sauce or lemon curd intensifies the lemon flavour greatly without really interrupting the smooth consistency.

TO MAKE THE LEMON CAKE

1. Preheat the oven to 350°F.

2. Cream together the sugar and butter until light and fluffy.

3. Add the egg and beat well.

4. Beat in the vanilla extract and lemon zest.

5. In a separate bowl, sift together the flour and baking powder.

6. Add the dry ingredients alternately with the milk, beginning and ending with the dry ingredients. In general, I add the dry ingredients in 3 portions and the milk in 2 portions.

7. Drop the batter by rounded tablespoons, closely together, all over the surface of the lemon sauce.

8. Once all the batter is in the dish, you can gently smooth out the surface of the batter with the back of a spoon.

9. Bake for 40-45 minutes or until a wooden toothpick inserted into the centre comes out clean.

10. Let the pudding sit for about 15 minutes to cool down slightly and let the sauce thicken a little.

11. Serve in cereal-sized bowls or dessert dishes.

Strawberry Pie

PREP TIME **40 MINUTES** | COOK TIME **30 MINUTES** | SERVES **10-12**

Our family's love affair with strawberry desserts took firm hold in this beautiful pie.

This Southern-style pie is often made using boxed strawberry gelatin powder. I set out to create a version with no artificial colours or flavours.

Why interfere with the sweet natural flavour of summer ripe strawberries? The real thing is always better. This pie is just perfect for peak summer strawberry season.

**FOR THE PASTRY
(MAKES 2 PIE SHELLS)**

3   cups all-purpose flour

½   tsp salt

¾   cup very cold butter

¼   cup very cold shortening
     (you can use additional
     butter, if you prefer)

¼   cup ice water

FOR THE STRAWBERRY FILLING

2   tsp unflavoured
     gelatin powder, stirred
     into ¼ cup cold water

6   cups sliced strawberries,
     divided in half

¾   cup sugar (use up to
     1¼ cups if you prefer
     it sweeter)

¼   cup water

2   tbsp cornstarch,
     dissolved in ¼ cup
     water

FOR THE WHIPPED CREAM

1   cup whipping cream

2   rounded tbsp icing
     sugar (powdered sugar)

1   tsp vanilla extract

TO MAKE THE PASTRY

1.   Using a food processor or a pastry blender, cut cold butter and shortening into the flour and salt until mixture resembles a coarse meal. Small pieces of butter should still be visible.

2.   Pour cold water over the mixture and work in by tossing with a fork until dough begins to form. Use your hands as little as possible and work the dough as little as possible.

3.   Divide dough into 2 balls, flatten into 2 rounds, wrap in plastic wrap, and place in the refrigerator to rest for a minimum of 20 minutes. You can freeze the second round for another time.

note > You can make your dough the previous day, but make sure you take it out of the fridge for 10-20 minutes to warm slightly before rolling out.

4.   Roll the dough into a 12-inch round and place in the bottom of a 9- or 10-inch pie plate.

5.   Trim and flute the edges as desired.

6.   Poke a few holes in the bottom of the pastry shell and place it in the refrigerator for an additional 20 minutes before baking at 400°F for 12-15 minutes or until golden brown. I prefer to blind bake this pastry shell to prevent shrinkage. To do so, line the pastry shell with aluminum foil or parchment paper and fill with baking weights or dried beans used as baking weights. Bake for 10 minutes then remove the weights and finish baking until golden brown.

7.   Cool completely before adding the filling.

TO MAKE THE FILLING

1. In a small saucepan, combine 3 cups of the sliced strawberries, sugar, and ¼ cup water and simmer for only a few minutes until the strawberries have released most of their juice.

2. Stir the cornstarch water into the simmering strawberries and stir constantly for 2-3 minutes while the strawberry mixture thickens.

3. Remove from heat and stir in the gelatin mixture until it is fully dissolved.

4. Allow to cool to almost room temperature before stirring in the remaining 3 cups of fresh sliced berries.

5. Pour into the baked pie shell and refrigerate for several hours or overnight until set.

TO MAKE THE VANILLA WHIPPED CREAM

1. Beat all of the ingredients together with an electric mixer until firm peaks form.

2. Use the cream to garnish the pie, or add a dollop to each slice of the pie when serving.

Coconut Cream Cheesecake

PREP TIME **25 MINUTES** | COOK TIME **1 HOUR 30 MINUTES** | SERVES **12-16**

Inspired by our decades-old coconut cream pie recipe from my first cookbook, this cheesecake takes on full coconut flavour with toasted coconut in both the crust and in the cheesecake batter. I use a combination of whipping cream and coconut milk to produce an incredibly creamy and smooth cheesecake. This indulgent dessert is always a knockout success when we're entertaining guests. It's sure to delight any coconut lover.

FOR THE COOKIE CRUMB CRUST

1⅓ cups graham cracker crumbs

⅓ cup butter, melted

¼ cup coconut, toasted, fine cut

3 tbsp sugar

FOR THE CHEESECAKE BATTER

1 eight-ounce packages of cream cheese (3 cups)

1 cup sugar

3 eggs

1 tsp vanilla extract

1 tsp coconut extract (optional)

¾ cup coconut milk (not cream of coconut)

¼ cup whipping cream

½ cup coconut, toasted, fine cut

FOR THE COCONUT WHIPPED CREAM (TO GARNISH)

¾ cup whipping cream

1½ tbsp icing sugar (powdered sugar)

¼ tsp coconut extract, or vanilla extract

1. First, toast 1 cup of fine dried (desiccated) coconut.

to toast the coconut > Preheat the oven to 325°F and sprinkle the coconut evenly in the bottom of an 8- or 9-inch baking pan. Bake for about 5 minutes or until lightly golden brown. Give the coconut a toss at least once to make sure that it browns evenly. Watch it closely. Dried coconut does still contain coconut oil, and it can burn quickly once it's toasted.

2. When the coconut is toasted, reduce the heat of the oven to 300°F for the cheesecake.

TO MAKE THE COOKIE CRUMB CRUST

1. In a small bowl, combine the graham cracker crumbs, melted butter, ¼ cup of the toasted coconut, and sugar.

2. Press the crumb mixture into the bottom of a lightly greased or parchment-lined 9-inch springform pan. Parchment paper is ideal here because it makes it very easy to release the cheesecake from the bottom of the pan. No need to grease the pan at all if you are using parchment paper. If you don't have parchment, grease the bottom only.

note > Wrap the outside of the springform pan with a double or triple layer of aluminum foil. This performs two functions: buffering the direct heat to the pan so that the cheesecake bakes more evenly; and secondly, it will catch any butter from the crust that may leak out while baking and hit the bottom of your oven. Preventing a smokey kitchen is always good!

TO MAKE THE CHEESECAKE BATTER

1. Cream together the cream cheese and sugar for 2-3 minutes until well combined.

2. Add the eggs, one at a time, beating well after each addition.

3. Beat in the vanilla extract and the coconut extract, if using.

4. Mix together the coconut milk and the ¼ cup whipping cream and add it to the cheesecake batter, blending well until the batter is very smooth.

5. Using a rubber spatula, scrape the bottom and sides of the bowl as well as the electric beaters/paddle, then give the batter a final beating for 1 minute on a higher speed. This final step ensures that there are no lumps in the batter and introduces a little air into the cheesecake to make it lighter.

6. Finally, stir in the ½ cup toasted coconut.

7. Pour the cheesecake batter over the prepared base and bake for about 90 minutes. (Oven temperatures will vary slightly. Mine takes the full 90 minutes.) Don't be a compulsive oven door opener! Don't open it at all in the first hour. The cheesecake does not have to brown at all in order to be fully baked; when the cake is properly baked, the surface of the cheesecake will lose any shine. It can still be slightly wobbly just at the centre at this point.

8. Remove the cake from the oven and run a sharp knife completely around the edge of the pan. This will allow for the cheesecake to shrink as it cools and should prevent it from cracking.

9. Allow the cheesecake to cool thoroughly on a wire rack at room temperature, not in the fridge. Refrigerate only after fully cooled.

TO MAKE THE COCONUT WHIPPED CREAM

1. Whip together the whipping cream, icing sugar, and coconut extract until firm peaks form.

2. Use the cream to garnish the edges of the cheesecake, and sprinkle on the remaining toasted coconut.

Black Forest Pie

PREP TIME **40** MINUTES | CHILL TIME **4** HOURS | SERVES **12-16**

The classic Black Forest dessert gâteau, reimagined in pie form! This is an easy, creamy, chocolatey, and very slightly boozy pie, with cherries soaked in cherry brandy overnight.

This chilled pie is an ideal choice for hot summer days to end a fantastic backyard barbecue meal. No worries, you can easily make an alcohol-free version as well, if you prefer.

FOR THE PASTRY (MAKES 2 PIE SHELLS)

2½ cups flour

1 cup very cold butter, cut into small cubes

½ tsp salt

¼ cup ice water (adding only enough to make a dough form)

FOR CHOCOLATE MOUSSE FILLING

4 cups whipping cream

2 cups dark chocolate chips

4 rounded tbsp icing sugar (powdered sugar)

2 tsp vanilla extract

YOU WILL ALSO NEED

2 cups fresh cherries, pitted

4 oz cherry brandy

1.   First, marinate the cherries in the cherry brandy overnight. Drain off the cherries but don't discard the brandy. Use this to create a cocktail, to add to something like a Chocolate Strawberry Trifle, or to add to a pitcher of sangria! Of course you can omit the brandy altogether for an alcohol-free version of this pie.

TO MAKE THE PASTRY

1.   Using a food processor or a pastry blender, cut cold butter into the flour and salt until mixture resembles a coarse meal. Small pieces of butter should still be visible.

2.   Pour cold water over the mixture and work in by tossing with a fork until dough begins to form. Use your hands as little as possible and work the dough as little as possible.

3.   Divide dough into 2 balls, flatten into 2 rounds, wrap in plastic wrap, and place in the refrigerator to rest for a minimum of 20 minutes. You can freeze the second round for another time.

note > You can make your dough the previous day, but make sure you take it out of the fridge for 10-20 minutes to warm slightly before rolling out.

4.   Roll the dough into a 12-inch round and place in the bottom of a 9- or 10-inch pie plate.

5.   Trim and flute the edges as desired.

6.   Poke a few holes in the bottom of the pastry shell and place it in the refrigerator for an additional 20 minutes before baking at 400°F for 12-15 minutes or until golden brown. I prefer to blind bake this pastry shell to prevent shrinkage. To do so, line the pastry shell with aluminum foil or parchment paper and fill with baking weights or dried beans used as baking weights. Bake for 10 minutes then remove the weights and finish baking until golden brown.

7. Cool completely before adding the filling.

TO MAKE THE CHOCOLATE MOUSSE FILLING

1. In a double boiler, melt the chocolate chips in ¾ cup of the whipping cream. Stir constantly as you melt the chocolate, and don't let it overheat. As soon as the last of the chocolate melts, take it off the heat and let it cool down to lukewarm.

2. Whip the remaining 3¼ cups cream with the icing sugar and vanilla to firm peaks. Remove roughly ⅓ of the whipped cream to a small bowl and reserve it to top the pie at the end.

3. By hand, fold the melted chocolate into the remaining, larger portion of the whipped cream. Be as gentle as you can so as not to deflate the cream.

to construct the pie >

1. Spoon half of the chocolate mixture into the baked pie shell and level it out.

2. Add the cherries on their sides, not with the holes from pitting sticking up. This makes for a better-looking presentation when cut.

3. Add the second half of the chocolate mixture to the pie and level that off as well.

4. Finally, garnish with the reserved whipped cream around the edge of the pie.

5. Chill for several hours before serving.

note > This is a large pie meant to feed 10 or more people. I have a large, deep 10-inch pie plate that I use for pies like these. If using shallower 8- or 9-inch pans, you will get 2 pies from this recipe. You may need to soak a few more cherries too. Just line the bottoms of the two pans with a single layer of cherries before starting the pie. This will tell you exactly how many you will need.

Almond Plum Cake

PREP TIME **20 MINUTES** | COOK TIME **40 MINUTES** | SERVES **8-10**

This recipe was inspired by my neighbour Elisabeth, who always seems to be looking for seasonal prune plums, which can be difficult to find here in Newfoundland. She is right to insist that these little plums are the perfect choice for an upside-down cake. Here I've chosen to flavour the cake with almond to complement the plums even more. The result is an easy and delicious dessert, best served warm with good vanilla bean ice cream.

FOR THE PLUM LAYER

½	cup butter, melted
⅓	cup brown sugar
1	tsp vanilla bean paste or vanilla extract
12	prune plums, or enough to cover the bottom of a 9x9-inch pan

FOR THE CAKE LAYER

2	cups flour
1	cup sugar
¾	cup ground almonds
2½	tsp baking powder
¾	cup milk
¼	cup butter, melted
¼	cup vegetable oil
2	eggs
1	tsp vanilla extract
½	tsp almond extract

TO MAKE THE PLUM LAYER

1. Mix together the melted butter, brown sugar, and vanilla.

2. Spread evenly on the bottom of a lightly greased 9x9-inch baking pan.

3. Cut the prune plums in half and remove the pits.

4. Lay the plums cut-side down on top of the butter and brown sugar mixture.

TO MAKE THE CAKE LAYER

1. Preheat the oven to 350°F (325°F for glass bakeware).

2. In the bowl of an electric mixer, blend together the flour, sugar, almonds, and baking powder.

3. Add the milk, melted butter, oil, eggs, vanilla extract, and almond extract all at once.

4. Blend on slow speed, just until the liquid ingredients are incorporated, and then on high speed for only about 20 seconds. Do not over-mix.

5. Quickly spread the batter evenly over the prepared plums.

6. Bake for about 40-45 minutes or until a toothpick inserted in the centre comes out clean.

7. Let rest in the pan for 10 minutes, then invert onto a serving platter or wire rack to cool off.

8. Serve with whipped cream or vanilla bean ice cream, with toasted almonds as a garnish.

White Chocolate Cheesecake Trifle
with Summer Fruit

PREP TIME **1 HOUR** | COOK TIME **45** MINUTES | SERVES **16** OR MORE

4   oz cherry brandy (optional)

6   cups assorted fresh fruit
     and berries

FOR THE SPONGE CAKE

6   eggs, large or extra-large
     (room temperature is best)

1   cup white sugar

1   tbsp vanilla extract

1   cup flour, sifted

2   tbsp salted butter, melted

**FOR THE WHITE CHOCOLATE
CHEESECAKE MOUSSE**

1⅓ cups whipping cream,
     split into 1 cup and ⅓ cup
     portions

1½ cups white chocolate chips

2   rounded tbsp icing sugar
     (powdered sugar)

2   tsp vanilla extract

1   cup (8 oz) cream cheese

FOR THE VANILLA WHIPPED CREAM

⅔   cup whipping cream

1½ tbsp icing sugar (powdered
     sugar)

½   tsp vanilla extract

Trifles have been a favourite dessert of mine since childhood. Perhaps their versatility and my never-ending imagination for combinations of flavours are what keep me coming back to them time after time.

This trifle features light as air sponge cake soaked with cherry brandy, then layered with a creamy white chocolate cheesecake mousse and all the luscious summer fruits and berries you can find. Sure to be an instant hit at any summer get-together.

TO MAKE THE SPONGE CAKE

1.   Preheat the oven to 325°F. Line the bottom of a 9-inch springform pan with parchment paper, but do not grease the sides. Greasing the sides will not allow the cake to rise well. Since the cake is cooled in the pan, the ungreased sides also provide support for the cake as it cools so that it will not shrink.

2.   In the bowl of an electric mixer, using a whisk attachment, combine the eggs, sugar, and vanilla extract, and beat on medium-high speed for about 10 minutes until the mixture is foamy and pale in colour.

3.   Reduce the speed of the mixer to medium-low, and with the mixer running, continuously sprinkle in rounded tablespoons of the flour. Stop the mixer as soon as the flour is fully incorporated.

4.   Remove 1-2 cups of the sponge cake batter and mix it with the melted butter.

5.   Immediately add this mixture back into the main batter, folding it in very gently with a rubber spatula. Make sure the butter mixture is fully mixed in, but be careful not to over-mix the batter when folding, as this can cause the batter to deflate.

6.   Pour the batter into the prepared pan and bake for approximately 45 minutes, or until the top springs back fully when pressed lightly. Watch this cake closely as it will over-bake easily if left for 5 minutes too long. Start checking it at the 40-minute mark just to be sure, although it always takes the full 45 minutes in my oven.

7.   Cool the cake completely IN THE PAN for at least a couple of hours before carefully and slowly running a sharp knife around the outside edge of the pan to release the cake from the sides.

8.   Release the sides of the springform pan and peel the parchment paper off the bottom of the cake.

9.   Using a sharp serrated knife, cut the cake into small cubes.

TO MAKE THE WHITE CHOCOLATE CHEESECAKE MOUSSE
1.   Heat the ⅓ cup whipping cream almost to boiling and pour over the white chocolate chips in a small bowl or measuring cup.

2.   Allow to stand for 5 minutes before stirring until smooth.

3.   Meanwhile, beat the 1 cup of whipping cream together with the icing sugar and vanilla extract until soft peaks form.

4.   Remove whipped cream from the bowl and set aside. Add the cream cheese to the mixer bowl and beat to soften it before mixing in the melted white chocolate.

5.   Finally, fold the whipped cream into this mixture. Do it gently to keep the mousse light.

CONTINUED ON PAGE 228 >

to construct the trifle >

1. First, reserve the best-looking fruits and berries to garnish the top of the trifle.

2. Add half of the cake cubes to the bottom of a large trifle dish (3 quart-size or larger). I like to fit them in neatly, so they take up less space.

3. Next, sprinkle the cake layer with a couple of ounces of the cherry brandy.

4. Add half of the fruit followed by a layer of half of the cheesecake mixture.

5. Repeat the layers.

6. Beat the ⅔ cup of whipping cream together with the icing sugar and vanilla extract to make the vanilla whipped cream.

7. Pipe a border of whipped cream around the edge of the trifle, or just dollop tablespoons of the whipped cream around the edge of the bowl.

8. Garnish with the reserved fruits and berries.

9. Chill for several hours before serving.

Screechin' Peach Cobbler

PREP TIME **30** MINUTES | COOK TIME **45** MINUTES | SERVES **8** OR MORE

This recipe is inspired by a bourbon peach cobbler that I had in the southern US several years back that I just couldn't forget. I asked myself how I could make it with a more local flavour.

The answer came from my favourite Niagara peaches combined with a local favourite rum.

The cobbler in this recipe is particularly light and delicious. However, the addition of our famous Newfoundland Screech dark rum to the peaches brings this recipe to a whole new level. Outstanding!

FOR THE PEACH MIXTURE

8-10	cups fresh peaches, peeled and cut into wedges
½	cup brown sugar
½	cup Screech (or other dark rum)
¼	cup butter, melted
2	tbsp cornstarch
½	tsp cinnamon
¼	tsp fresh nutmeg, grated

FOR THE COBBLER DOUGH

1½	cups flour
½	cup sugar
2	tsp baking powder
½	tsp salt
½	cup very cold butter, cut in small pieces
¾	cup whipping cream
1	tsp vanilla extract

TO MAKE THE PEACH MIXTURE

1. Preheat the oven to 350°F. Toss together the peaches, brown sugar, rum, butter, cornstarch, cinnamon, and nutmeg, and spread in the bottom of a deep-dish 9x13-inch (or similar sized) glass baking pan.

2. Cover with aluminum foil and bake for 20 minutes.

3. While the fruit is baking, prepare the cobbler topping.

TO MAKE THE COBBLER DOUGH

1. In a food processor combine the flour, sugar, baking powder, and salt.

2. Using the pulse button on the food processor, cut in the butter. Pulse until the mixture resembles a coarse meal. If you don't own a food processor, you can cut the butter into the flour mixture using a pastry cutter or even a couple of knives between the fingers.

3. To the flour/butter mixture add the whipping cream and vanilla extract, folding in the cream just until a soft dough forms. Do not overwork the dough or it will become too tough. Less is more here, and the less you work the dough, the lighter your cobbler will turn out.

tip > For extra flavour penetration, you can first soak the peaches in the rum for a couple of hours or overnight.

4. Drop the cobbler dough in heaping tablespoonfuls onto the hot fruit mixture.

5. Return the baking pan to the oven for about another 25-35 minutes or until the top is evenly golden brown.

6. Let the cobbler rest for 10-15 minutes before serving warm with some good French vanilla ice cream.

index

acknowledgements

None of the successes I've enjoyed over the past thirteen years have come without help, inspiration, and encouragement. I am grateful to everyone who has played even the smallest part of making them happen.

I must say thank you to all of the visitors to my website and those who have bought my previous cookbooks. You are what makes *Rock Recipes* possible.

Again, to the terrific team at Breakwater Books, thanks for making the process of publishing a book so painless. In particular, thanks to Rhonda Molloy who has now designed all five of my cookbooks. Your patience and talent are appreciated. Also, many thanks to Jocelyne Thomas and Marianne Ward for making the editing process easy, at a time when I have so many irons in so many fires.

Once more, much love and appreciation to Lynn, the unsung hero of *Rock Recipes*. To catalogue all she does would cover more than this entire page.

Much gratitude to my entire extended family, plus Mom and Dad. So many of you have been part of my culinary influence in a thousand little ways. That kid you encouraged to keep cooking really appreciates it.

And finally, to Olivia and Noah who grew up with *Rock Recipes* as part of our family life and (almost) always were patient while dinner had to be photographed before it was eaten.

They were eight and nine years old when this all started. Now, Olivia has graduated from university and is out in the working world, while Noah follows his passion for photography at university in Nova Scotia. Your mom and I are proud of you both, every single day, as you take on the world.

One wife, two kids, one mortgage, lifelong food obsessive, recipe blogger, and food photographer: that's how *Rock Recipes* creator Barry C. Parsons describes himself on *RockRecipes.com*. Called "one of the best food blogs in Canada" by the *National Post*, and ranked by Feedspot.com as the number one food blog in Canada, *RockRecipes.com* boasts over 650,000 social media followers from around the world, with millions of online visitors monthly. The popularity of his recipes and cooking philosophy has led to four incredibly successful cookbooks: *Rock Recipes*, *Rock Recipes 2*, *Rock Recipes Cookies*, and *Rock Recipes Christmas*. Parsons cooks & writes from his home in St. John's, NL.

Find more from Barry at www.RockRecipes.com

 /RockRecipes   @RockRecipes   🅿 /RockRecipes